—— **ENGLIS**
THROU
DRAMA

— ENGLISH —
THROUGH
DRAMA

David Eccles

HUTCHINSON
London   Sydney   Auckland   Johannesburg

Hutchinson Education
An imprint of Century Hutchinson Ltd
62–65 Chandos Place
London WC2N 4NW

Century Hutchinson Australia Pty Ltd
89–91 Albion Street, Surry Hills,
New South Wales 2010, Australia

Century Hutchinson New Zealand Limited
PO Box 40-086, Glenfield, Auckland 10,
New Zealand

Century Hutchinson South Africa (Pty) Ltd
PO Box 337, Bergvlei, 2012 South Africa

First published 1989

Set in Bembo
by Hope Services Ltd., Abingdon
Printed and bound in Great Britain by
Mackays of Chatham PLC, Chatham, Kent

British Library Cataloguing in Publication Data
Eccles, David
  English through drama.
  1. Secondary school. Curriculum subjects: English
  literature. Teaching. Role of drama
  I. Title
820′.7′12

  ISBN 0–09–175847–5

Contents

What is this book about and who is it for?

At a simple level this book is about the various ways in which drama can support and enhance work in the English classroom. It is not a theoretical text, though I hope the philosophy which underpins the various approaches will come across via the descriptions of activities. For many English teachers, drama is an integral part of their teaching and may even exist as a time-tabled slot in the week; what this book aims to do is to offer all teachers concrete examples and starting points which can be used as part of the reading, writing, listening and talking activities in the classroom.

The activities described are not offered as 'models' or lesson plans to follow, but as practical accounts of possible ways of working in a classroom. The various chapters cover ways of using drama with G.C.S.E. texts, strategies to provoke responsive reading and the development of a personal understanding of class readers, the use of drama to stimulate oral and written work, and the promotion of affective learning experiences in which personal meaning is refined through a shared, collaborative experience.

The descriptions of lessons are offered in a variety of forms – some are plans, some are loose frameworks, some are retrospective accounts, some are anecdotal. There are descriptions of individual lessons (one-offs), of lesson sequences interwoven with evaluation and planning processes, of extended projects, and of activities that use drama as part of a whole half-term's work on a theme or novel.

I would hope that anyone reading (or dipping into) this book would find useful, practical ideas and suggestions that could be tried out in their own classrooms – but ultimately no book can tell you how to teach, and you will have to find your own ways to adapt the strategies to suit your own situation and your own classes. This book, then, is a means of sharing ways of working that have all been tried and tested in the field, and found to be successful.

For some teachers the word drama conjures up visions of rowdy disruptive pupils engaged in mock fights or else groups inventing superficial and pointless little playlets. My own vision of drama is of the creation of a feeling experience, achieved through taking on a role and exploring that role in a context which is different from one's own. I have been considerably influenced by the work of Heathcote

1

and Bolton, and by the concept of 'internal action' which is designed to bring about a shift in attitude, with physical action relegated to a minor (though still important) role. 'Acting out' – a common preconception of drama – may in fact be sitting and talking, but unlike ordinary classroom discussion this is done *in role*. Less physical action means more reliance on words and an emphasis on thinking and feeling, which in turn mean that all the activities that are described in ensuing chapters can be done *in an ordinary classroom*. I will return to a deeper consideration of the term 'in-role' in the opening chapter, as it is a concept fundamental to the kinds of drama activities described in the book; suffice it to say that one does not need specialist space, drama expertise or acting skills in order to facilitate this kind of work – all it requires is a willingness to try something new, a realisation that there is no recipe for 'instant success', and a commitment to allowing pupils to share (and even determine) the direction of the work.

The National Curriculum English Working Group re-affirmed the place of drama in the curriculum in its report:

> 'Drama is also of crucial importance as a learning medium, for example, in promoting collaborative talk, extending language skills and awareness of language in use, in assisting the development of voice skills in relation to reading aloud, and in extending both the form and the content of children's own writing. Drama is not simply a subject, but also – more importantly – a method; it is both a creative art form in its own right and also a learning tool. Furthermore, drama is one of the key ways in which children can gain an understanding of themselves and of others, can gain confidence in themselves as decision-makers and problem-solvers, can learn to function collaboratively, and can explore – within a supportive framework – not only a range of human feelings, but also a whole spectrum of social situations and/or moral dilemas.'
>
> *[English for ages 5 to 11]*

What then are the connections between English and Drama?

1

English and Drama

How do they complement each other?

Rationale

Drama and English are often seen as having their own distinct and separate content. There is sometimes a kind of uneasy relationship between the two and in some cases no real connection at all. However, both Her Majesty's Inspectorate and the Bullock report have drawn English teachers' attention to the role drama plays in language development:-

'Drama will supply, often vividly and memorably, some of the contexts and situations in which language does occur. It is capable of increasing an understanding of language, and encouraging co-operative work in language.'

[Aspects of Secondary Education]

'It is improvisation, involving the complex relationships between the written and the spoken word, which seems to have particular value for language development.'

[A Language for Life]

Since drama will give rise to situations which enforce speech, then there is an obvious and accessible connection that many English teachers recognise and exploit. Drama provides an infinite variety of situations which will require specific language uses – to inform and instruct, to negotiate and mediate, to reason and logically persuade, to report – and the talk (and writing) will not be in isolation but embedded in the situation, and subject to modification imposed by working in a group. By working in role, pupils are given a semi-real context for oral and written tasks and so the process of language development takes place more purposefully.

Research into the nature of English teaching has highlighted that what is distinctive about English, as opposed to many other subjects, is that a large proportion of the knowledge comes to the classroom with the child, rather than with the teacher. The mechanisms that operate in an English lesson are designed to relate the subject to what the pupils already know or think. In other words the 'content' of English is the knowledge that has come in a random or fragmented way, in unplanned and unstructured situations that form a child's experiences of living in the world. English is 'about working on the knowledge we have acquired from the unsystematic processes of living, about giving expression to it, and making it into a firmer and more conscious kind of knowledge.' [Peter Medway, *Finding a Language*.] The study of literature is at the centre of this work, since literature is knowledge in action: the process of writing can be viewed as a way of looking into the self and making conscious what the writer already knows at an unconscious level. Not only the words, but what lies behind the words is important, and pupils' own existing knowledge is displayed by being brought to bear on particular real or imagined situations. We learn from literature in the same sort of way that we learn from working over our own 'first-order' experience, and in reading a work of fiction pupils will be both inside and outside the experience.

Literature also uses language in a highly specialised way, in order to refine and intensify our responses to experience. An H.M.I.'s report notes that: 'Through his encounters with literature the pupil should appreciate the rich possibilities of choice in language and some of the most important purposes which language choice can serve . . . [among the responses is] relating the vision and intention of the writer to the language he uses'. [*Aspects of Secondary Education*] Literature, with its complex and specific uses of language, plays an important part in developing an understanding of, and a response to, language.

Both drama and literature are concerned with explorations of human behaviour which are then tested against the participant's or reader's own experiences: a writer enables her reader to look at life through the eyes of another; drama allows the participant to experience this actively.

> 'Through the process of identifying, readers give life to texts, in this sense reading is akin to role-playing in drama . . . like role-play, identifying as a reader releases a fund of subjective experiences and recalled information that aids understanding and appreciation.'
>
> [B.J. Wagner, *Drama as a Learning Medium*]

In improvisation you are required to share parts of your experiences of life and to express these in movement and speech. In other words, you bring what you know to the front and share it in a personal and direct way. This same process is in operation when we read a novel – what Bullock terms 'responsive reading' – and when we read a novel with a class we share our experiences and responses in the same way that we do in improvisation. Information retained about characters, events or issues is often meaningless without personal response, and it is here that the drama process offers a unique contribution – the affective experience as well as the cognitive experience. 'For them to understand, the pupils have to find a way of almost recreating what was inside a writer's head' [D. Jackson,

Talking and Writing About Literature] – a process Stratta, Wilkinson and Dixon call 'imaginative recreation'.

English and drama, then, share common central concerns:

'What is known must in fact be brought to life afresh in every knower by his own efforts.'

[*A Language for Life*]

'Drama enables children to understand what they already know, but do not yet know they know.'

[D. Heathcote, *Drama in Context*]

By combining approaches to reading and responding to a novel with the drama process, we are enabling children to share in an active and meaningful way the inner world into which they enter when reading – which is then elaborated and enriched by the group experience so that 'by joining together reading and drama, students can combine interest in the lives of the characters in the story with an inner exploration of themselves and their own struggles for control over their own lives'. [Booth & Hains *Story Drama*].

Heathcote, when defining improvisation, said, 'dramatic improvisation means putting yourself in other people's shoes, and by using personal experience to help you understand their point of view, you may discover you knew more than when you started'. [*Improvisation*] The drama process is a shared process, in which pupils exist as people inside the metaphor of the situation they are exploring, and yet are still themselves, bringing their own experiences, impressions and knowledge to bear upon the situation they create. These explorations are active and interactive – unlike reading which is passive and personal – and it is this 'active involvement and identification with a fictitious situation which is unique to drama'. [O'Neill *et al.*, *Drama Guidelines*] Talking and writing are ways of reflecting, ordering and clarifying experiences; drama complements and enriches these active explorations in a unique way.

What then are the kinds of outcomes we aim for by bringing together drama and English? The objectives are:

● to stimulate a desire to read (or read on)

● to go beyond what is on the surface – to look behind words at implications

● to provide a context for language development and simultaneously offer a model of rich, conscious language use

● to offer pupils who may have problems with the written word a vehicle which allows them to express their feelings and responses

5

confidently and imaginatively (i.e. to provide opportunities for learning through talking and feeling)

● to provide new learning contexts and teacher-pupil relationships which hand over the responsibility for decisions and question forming and answering to the pupils

● to provide a group experience for the sharing of personal responses, in order to enrich individual responses by awakening in pupils awareness of the possible range and variety of response

● to create opportunity for affective experience so that understanding is personal and felt, not something given to pupils by the teacher

● to use situations embedded in pupils' own lives so that they are able to apply their own knowledge to understand or probe the complexities of a story's themes and characters

● to consolidate information acquired about character, motivation or incidents from the reading of a novel or story

● to bring together what pupils know or have picked up from a story-line or characterisation so that they can predict developments, compare these with what actually happens and consider the author's intentions and choices

● to examine social and moral issues from a personal standpoint, which may lead to modification or justification of personal values

● to make the reading of a book enjoyable and memorable

● to provide concrete experiences to enrich or stimulate purposeful talking and writing

● to provide a sense of audience through an 'as-if' context which gives writing, reading, listening and talking activities a purpose within a coherent framework.

Obviously the drama mode will simultaneously affect the social climate of the group, and trust, confidence, tolerance, understanding, responsibility, negotiation, co-operation, awareness of self and others will form a background of more long-term aims; in the same way language development will have specific aims in specific lessons – vocabulary, reporting, using appropriate register and tone, negotiation, persuasion, informing, synthesising and so on.

The drama process and working in role

What is involved in the 'drama process', and how does a teacher engage pupils with it? The most essential feature of the drama-process is role-play. By this I mean a pupil taking on the role of someone other than herself, and then interacting with others (also in role) to explore a situation as if they were those people, or had some of the attitudes and feelings of those people. I do not mean extensive and deep characterisation, with a concentration on body movement, gesture, accent, etc. – though this may grow naturally as the pupil grows in her role.

Sometimes the pupil may be herself, but in an entirely different situation. This type of role-play offers pupils who are relatively inexperienced in role work a confident and secure base from which to tackle other roles; it also allows a pupil to explore, as herself, an unfamiliar situation. A novel will often deal with a situation removed from a pupil's own experience, and it is sometimes necessary to prepare the way for an understanding of that experience. For example, in some introductory sessions to *Lord of the Flies*, fourth year pupils became fourth year pupils in the imaginary situation of a survival holiday where they were suddenly and unexpectedly left to cope on their own. Immediately questions of leadership, rules, survival and social organisation had to be confronted – as indeed they have to be confronted by the boys in *Lord of the Flies*.

When a pupil takes on the role of someone other than herself, she will bring something of herself into the creation of that role, and draw upon her own experience or understanding. This type of role-play offers particularly fertile ground, since the pupil assessing a situation as if she were someone else is moving toward the articulation of new understanding. Role-play allows the pupil to be spectator and participant at the same time – and she speaks as if she were inside the fictional situation, calling upon her own ideas and experiences, and shaping them as she does so into a conscious articulation – a very different process from a discussion carried out in an objective manner.

Pupils–in–role

It is not enough merely to say, 'You are a council tenant living in a damp flat. It is rumoured the Council are about to condemn your block of flats. You are going to a meeting of all the tenants to discuss this'. Introduced in this way, role-play can easily degenerate into shallow or superficial talk and play-acting; for the drama to have any significance activities must be used which will probe more deeply and lead to a more subtle appreciation of the situation or people within the story. Strategies are needed which will help the pupils to grow into the roles they are building for themselves, and at the same time commit something of themselves to the situation. It becomes important – *it matters* – they discover Coleridge's 'willing suspension of disbelief', as Gavin Bolton puts it. Non-drama activities can be very useful here – painting or drawing pictures of their new homes; locating themselves on maps of a new environment; producing autobiographical sketches, lists of equipment they have with them or objects that are important to them and writing in role after some preliminary drama are all methods which help children grow in, and believe in, their roles. For example, in the introductory sessions on *Lord of the Flies* just referred to, pupils made a list of everything they had brought (which was private, and only shared if they felt important), and their own writing in role was later used to help recapture the scene at the start of the next phase.

Pair or small group work can help pupils find their way in and establish their roles: villagers discussing in pairs their memories of Dr Frankenstein, or in groups discussing their reactions to the arrival of Hannah Frankenstein, could be very useful exercises to introduce work on *Frankenstein's Aunt*. When working on *The White Mountains*, before the pupils took on roles as members of the Council of Elders, preliminary work was necessary to establish what living in the community was like, and what the problems of that community were. Alternative pair exercises to the role-play could have included swapping memories about the journey to the White Mountains, discussing what they missed most, or showing a new arrival around. (This is described fully in Chapter 7.)

Commitment to the drama at an individual and group level can sometimes be achieved by the use of a formalised ritual – the offering of gifts, a ceremonial welcome, or an oath of allegiance. Chapter 2 illustrates a way of approaching the drama using this strategy (in the section *The Traitor*), and a ritual was employed in work on *The White Mountains* – in this case as a way of tackling pupils' lack of involvement in a previous session (see Chapter 7).

If the teacher works in role herself, maintains seriousness, challenges, supports and questions, then opportunities to help build belief in the roles and the situation can be developed, while time is allowed for the pupil to grow in her role. This brings me straight to a very useful and important strategy – teacher-in-role.

Teacher-in-role

In this strategy the teacher takes a part in the drama – she is in role as well as the pupils. This means the teacher is inside the drama, with the pupils, and projecting attitudes which can be used in the service of the drama the pupils are creating. This enables her to put on pressures and create tensions when the need arises.

In the normal pattern of classroom activities, the teacher is usually the decision maker, the focal point, the repository of knowledge – even the dominator. But in the drama process, if the work is to have value, then the pupils must explore the situation, have the opportunity for initiating action and making decisions, and have time to reflect upon these decisions. Drama is a shared activity, and if the teacher is also a part of the learning process then the notions of sharing, exploring and reflecting can be made more natural. If we wish to encourage the development and articulation of personal responses, then we must refrain from telling children, and share our responses as they share theirs, in an atmosphere of mutual trust and respect. When the teacher is in role, she is in a position to direct and focus the learning from within, to challenge response (without threatening), to ensure children have the opportunity to seize the initiative, to help build belief in the situation, to unify or fragment the group – whatever is necessary or appropriate to deepen the drama without stopping the process and dominating from outside.

One advantage of being in role is that you are free to express attitudes that would never be accepted from a teacher: for example, when Beowulf musters his men and persuades them to come with him (see *Dragon-Slayer*), the teacher can, instead of being Beowulf, be a whining, snivelling coward. To ensure that there is no easy way out for Beowulf and his companions (e.g. not taking this person, or merely making derogatory remarks) it may be crucial that she be persuaded to join the expedition – perhaps she is an accomplished navigator, has been to Denmark before, or owns the fastest boat. This gives the pupils a problem to deal with. How will they persuade this person to come? Adopting this role yourself will allow you to exert pressure upon the group from within.

Teaching in role, then, is an immensely valuable strategy: at one level it creates new teacher–pupil relationships, not based on the normal classroom hierarchy, which create new opportunities for purposeful talk; at another level it enables the teacher to facilitate movement from superficial drama to the creation of a shared thinking and feeling experience. As the teacher is inside the drama she is also able to provide models of appropriate language, and to demonstrate that the work is serious.

Agreeing on and giving a clear signal for the group to recognise when the teacher is functioning in role (inside the drama), and when the teacher is 'teacher' (outside the drama) is very helpful when pupils are beginning this kind of work, as it is sometimes difficult for them to recognise and realise the implications. Signals can be very simple 'when I sit here I will be . . . when I pick up my clipboard I will be in role . . . when I walk into this area I will be in role – outside the circle I am teacher'. Once pupils accept the convention of teacher-in-role they will accept the teacher taking several different roles during the course of the lesson, provided the signals and context are clear.

The examples described in the following chapters make use of teacher-in-role to suit a variety of purposes – to clarify, to advise, to threaten, to question, to be taught, to appeal for help, to encourage reflection – all of which press pupils to respond at both a thinking and feeling level, as themselves but also in role, and through this engagement to move toward articulation of their thoughts and feelings.

The choice of teacher roles is enormous – each role being shaped by the specific purposes of that particular moment in the drama – but there are three broad categories worth distinguishing:

High status roles

The Chief, the Queen or King, the 'boss', the leader figure. For a teacher starting to work in role it is often easiest to take on a role with some degree of authority, which allows her to control the drama subtly from a position quite close to her normal teacher role. The high status role allows information to be imparted, organisation or 'ground rules' to be explained and the pupils in role to be confronted and challenged, but the teacher must be careful that the role does not dominate the pupils' opportunities for decision-making or questioning.

Middle status roles

This kind of role allows the teacher to initiate action and then step back leaving the pupils to control and direct the drama, e.g. the messenger who brings news and then leaves, the hotel clerk who has other pressing duties to deal with. These middle status roles shift the power to unseen authority, but still give the teacher access to work *with* the pupils. The 'Haunt-Away' project (described in Chapter 2) started with a high status role (the area manager) which became a middle status role when I had to inform the group of the board's decision – over which I had no control. The policeman who is just following orders, the council workman who is posting up planning notices or the Queen's representative are the kinds of role that give a teacher more room to manoeuvre (without polarising her position in relation to the pupils' roles) and can allow challenge or clarification of thinking in a non-threatening way.

Low status roles

Here the opportunity for initiation and control is firmly placed in the hands of the pupils. The teacher in the role of one who doesn't know anything, is frightened or needs help, will create a situation demanding a very different response. This kind of role can open up exciting possibilities since the teacher is not the one with answers or suggestions and she must rely on the group for sympathy, help, advice or support. The mother entering a battered wives refuge or the servant who doesn't understand the orders of his master are roles that require the pupils to respond to a teacher in ways they would not normally have to in school.

If one combines high and low status roles – e.g. a weak, ineffectual King, this in turn presents a whole new range of problems. How do you talk to your King (who has power and authority over you) when you know he is useless, indecisive and avoids facing problems?

The many different ways of using and working in role are described in the accounts of actual lessons in the following chapters, and the opening example in Chapter 2, *The H.D. Factor*, gives a clear account of introducing and starting work in this way, but there are some general points worth stressing.

● If the members of the group have not worked in this way before then the idea will need to be clearly explained and some ground rules established – how will pupils know when you are in role, that the drama has started, that there are times you will all step out of the drama to reflect upon what is happening? It may be useful to cue pupils in to listening carefully for clues as to role by giving a few practice examples – the village postlady who approaches a pupil saying 'Only two letters today Mrs Williams . . . how are you feeling then?' will quickly establish the fact that teacher is someone else and that teacher (in role) will interact with pupils (in role).

● Many groups find the idea of working in role rather unusual – and if the situation is at all threatening and alien to their normal expectations of classroom practice they may well giggle or be silly to hide their own embarrassment and uncertainty about what is expected of them. It may be necessary to stop the drama and talk about their response, or to press on maintaining personal commitment and seriousness, depending on how you judge their response. It you haven't worked in role before, it is often easiest to assume a high status role at the start, and the examples in Chapter 2 explore a variety of roles and how to introduce them.

● Going straight into role can move the group quickly into drama-mode – 'Right then, I hope you've brought all the items on the list . . .' but this way in will require the drama to be stopped quite soon to check on what pupils are picking up about context, your role, their role, etc. Sometimes however it's worth explaining what your role will be – 'when I come in I will be the council official who will show you where you will be temporarily rehoused during this emergency . . .'

(A comprehensive account of teaching in role appears in B.J. Wagner's *Drama as a Learning Medium*.)

Another person in role

The use of another person in role allows the teacher to facilitate the progress of the drama without having to step in and out of role – meaning that tension and belief can be more easily maintained. The teacher is freer to think on her feet as the drama progresses and can more easily observe what is happening and make decisions accordingly. There can be problems finding a colleague who is free (and willing) at the right time, but the possibilities opened up are worth pursuing. Why not consider using a parent, a capable fifth or sixth former or even the Head or Deputy? Drama or English Advisers may also be willing to come in and work alongside you.

Another person can provide the focus for the drama – perhaps becoming a character in a novel whom the group is to question, the managing director who has come to hear about workers' attitudes to computerised technology, or the person who may be willing to finance an expedition. I once had an advisory teacher role-play a foreign dissident who had illegally smuggled himslf into the country but who had been picked up by local police. The pupils were in role as doctors, police, social workers and Home Office officials – all they knew was that there was a man whose possessions were obviously foreign (these were available for them to study), who had been picked up wandering the streets at night, and who refused to communicate with anyone. The man spoke no English (or appeared not to), was very frightened, and unwilling to co-operate. After observing him in the cell via a 'hidden video-camera', pupils had then to establish contact, get him to trust them, communicate with him, and deal with the Russian Ambassador demanding his return!

References

Booth & Hains, 'Story Drama' in *2D*, vol. 1 no. 2.

D.E.S., *A Language for Life*, H.M.S.O. 1975 [The Bullock Report]

D.E.S., *Aspects of Secondary Education*, H.M.S.O., 1978

Heathcote, Dorothy, 'Improvisation' in *Drama in Education*, vol. 1 no. 3

Heathcote, Dorothy, 'Drama in Context' in *Exploring Theatre and Education*, ed. Robinson, Hutchinson, 1982

Jackson, D., 'Talking and Writing about Literature' in *Language Teaching and Learning*, ed. M. Torbe, Ward Lock, 1981

Medway, Peter, *Finding a Language*, Chameleon Press, 1980

O'Neill *et al.*, *Drama Guidelines*, Hutchinson, 1978

Wagner, B.J., *Drama as a Learning Medium*, Hutchinson, 1979

2

Drama and Language

How can I see what I think till I hear what I say?
Alice in Wonderland

Rather than continue with theory or descriptions of strategies without a context, I want to move on to consider some practical examples which illustrate the processes of English through drama. This chapter explores how role play can create opportunities for language development as an integral part of mainstream English work. All the activities can lead to written work which is more informed as a result of the thinking and feeling experience of being in role.

1   The H.D. factor

The previous chapter explored the strategy of the teacher taking on a role and working within the drama alongside the pupils. This lesson offers a secure starting point from which to try out this strategy, since initially the teacher operates in a role very similar to her normal teacher role (organiser, information-giver, stimulus-provider). Subsequently the teacher moves into a different kind of role (although this is still straightforward and does not need any special skills).

The lesson does not require the pupils to 'act' or even move about. Drama *can* mean sitting, talking and thinking – it is looking at the situation *as if* you were someone else that is the key!

Background

The lesson can easily be organised in any space or classroom and desks should be cleared and pupils seated on chairs in a circle. The teacher should form a part of that circle. It would be helpful if pupils had a pencil and notebook to hand.

The lesson can stand on its own, or could develop into a series of lessons. It has been used successfully across the full 11–18 age and ability range, since the pupils make the situation as sophisticated as they wish – first years have had bank robbers using the Big House, an A-level group decided the house was a secret germ warfare establishment! You will need to familiarise yourself totally with the suggested background before starting the lesson.

The role play is designed to encourage students to practise questioning skills; to assimilate and interpret information; to practise note-taking and recall skills; to evaluate and hypothesise; and to

13

organise information in a variety of written formats. Opportunities can be built in for pupils to negotiate and make key decisions about the work if you feel ready to hand over control of this area to the pupils (but you will have to face the consequences of this). If you are just embarking on this kind of work, it might be more appropriate to treat the lesson as a one-off introductory session leading into written tasks – in which case ignore the follow-up suggestions.

The lesson

1   Tell the pupils they will be doing some role-play work (I avoid the word drama at first when working with a new class). They will be 'investigative journalists'. Ask what this term means and establish agreed shared meaning. Ask what kind of things these reporters might investigate. Be prepared to suggest if necessary.

2   Ask the pupils to work in pairs (or turn to the person on their left) and, as reporters, tell each other about the investigation they have just been working on. Allow a few minutes thinking time, then give them a signal to start. If anyone can't think of anything, give them some help, e.g. illegal dog fighting; a con-man posing as a gasman; thefts of paintings of one artist.

3   Allow the activity to run for a few minutes and ensure that both partners have a chance to talk. Arrange the circle again and tell them you are going to take on the role of their editor who wants to hear how their stories are shaping up. Establish a signal to show when you are teacher and when you are editor (e.g. 'when I am holding this clipboard I am the editor, when it is on the floor I am teacher'). Remind them they are journalists not members of 3X and they should try to talk as such. You could even ask them to describe the room you are meeting in to help set the scene ('What does the room you meet me in look like? What is on the walls?) – but don't get side-tracked into specifying endless details – just a few suggestions will suffice. Tell them the meeting will begin when you give your signal.

4   Pick up your clipboard (or whatever) and talk to the class as if you are the editor. (Don't try to act, remember the guidance in the previous chapter.) Something like – 'Good morning everyone, thanks for coming at such short notice to this briefing meeting. I know you're all very busy but something's come up . . . first however I wonder if I could have an update on the stories you've been working on. Has anyone a story ready or almost ready to print?'

You may need to prompt if the class are not used to this way of working – 'Sarah – what was it you were working on? . . . Ah yes – how's it coming along?'

Try to allow five or six pupils to share their investigations and be

14

prepared to probe a little deeper – 'Did you have any special problems?', 'Were people willing to talk to you?'. This will help strengthen belief.

5   Now shift the focus to introduce the real reason you have called them together – e.g. 'Right, well there's a lot going on and I'm going to have to ask some of you to put your investigations on ice for a couple of days. I've got something that I think is very unusual and I'm not sure how to proceed. Let me tell you about it . . .'

You now have to sketch out the following points:
Tip-off received from a friend in the country that a murder appears to have been committed but the body seems to have vanished; reliable source but story seems odd; can't print till we're sure of the facts; my friend received information from Mr/s King that he/she had found a body and reported it but it has vanished; don't know much more but would like a couple of you to go down to this village – Wallton – and ferret about; see if you can persuade Mr/s King to give more details; my friend said Mr/s King was a bit 'odd and grumpy but a reliable sort'; he/she drinks in the village pub – the Black Horse – most evenings. Be prepared to elaborate but answer requests for more details with 'I don't know'. Your source will remain anonymous – journalistic prerogative.

6   Continue with 'Well that's all I know – what do you think?' Allow time for speculation *in role* and ask for two volunteers to go and interview Mr/s King. Ask other journalists about how this should be handled – will they need a cover story? How will they gain the witness's confidence? Keep this discussion firmly in role.

Break the drama by signalling you are now teacher again.

7   As teacher, explain the following organisational details – space in centre of circle will be the pub (place a couple of tables and chairs in it). When the two reporters arrive they will find one person in the pub (don't answer questions of identity). People in the circle are to 'eavesdrop' on the conversation and make notes on anything significant or interesting. Two key strategies need to be clearly explained:
– members of the 'audience' can interrupt the interview *at any time* and ask their own questions AS IF they were present.
– interviewers *OR* members of the audience can STOP the interview if they feel it isn't working or getting anywhere *at any time*, discuss it out of role and then go back and try again (if necessary right from the start). Interviewers may also stop the drama to ask audience for help and advice.

8   Place yourself in the pub, (you will now take on the role of Mr/s King). You have a very suspicious and mercenary attitude – respond to offers of a drink but make the reporters work hard to gain your trust – allow the story to be pieced together in a fragmentary way. If

the reporters are getting nowhere, be prepared to stop the drama and discuss what is happening out of role, before restarting at an appropriate point. When as much information as possible has been gleaned, then come out of role and break the drama.

The background material for the role of Mr/s King is at the end of the lesson notes.

9   Out of role discuss information gathered, attitude to Mr/s King and build an overall impression. Consider what gaps there are in the story.

(It is possible to stop at this point and set a written task – reporters to write a summary of what has been found out for the editor and suggest lines of further enquiry.)

10   Reconvene editorial meeting and discuss in role what action to take next. Do we believe Mr/s King? Any theories? What do we need to find out? How would we do it? What lines of enquiry should we pursue, remembering that we do not want any rivals to get wind of our scoop? How could we verify story without alerting anyone who might have something to hide?

(An alternative written task might be to ask reporters at this point to draft a preliminary lead article and headline based on information so far.)

The scheme could finish here or be followed up by allowing pupils to carry out investigations along the lines suggested in the last meeting and then producing a finished lead article.

[The inspiration and material for this lesson was the nursery rhyme 'Humpty Dumpty' – hence H.D. Factor, Wallton, pub name, location of body etc.!]

Possible developments

Should you feel it appropriate the following ways of continuing the scheme have been found effective with different classes:
● reporters continuing their investigations and reporting back to the editorial committee
● pupils in pairs or small groups as villagers in Wallton discussing how things have changed since the new owners took over the 'Big House'. A verbal sharing of key points will help build some background/provide new possibilities for the reporters.
● decide *out of role* what the 'story' is about and use this to work on new scenes/interviews. One class gave me the problem of how to use their decision that the house was H.Q. to drug smugglers – I cast them in role as police and posed the question, 'Why are they drawing attention to themselves? Something seems very odd here'.
● ask pupils to work in groups and reconstruct the events leading up to the murder and indicate a motive. Discuss the various scenes and

consider the possibilities/problems each one raises – but be prepared for quite an *active* session!

This lesson has controls built in and the two teacher roles are very straightforward, providing you are familiar with the background story. However you should feel free to improvise and just use the suggested background as a framework. If you find yourself unhappy or uncomfortable with the pub interview, try storming out in a huff (in role of course!) then discuss out of role why Mr/s King did that.

Sometimes you may be able to enlist the help of a colleague and work together collaboratively on planning and implementing schemes. While it is worth considering having another teacher to take on one of the roles, in practice I have found that pupils will easily accept you in any number of roles provided the signals are clear.

Background material for lesson

Mr/s King's story
You run a farm in Wallton, and have no surviving family. Two weeks ago, when travelling to work by tractor at dawn, you discovered a body at the foot of one of the walls surrounding the 'Big House'. The body had its head stoved in (improvise gory details if you wish). Description as you recall it – middle aged, bald, dark overcoat.

You reported this to the guards at the gate of the house; they said they would deal with it; you went back to get on with ploughing assuming they would tell the police.

On the way home the body was gone and everything was tidied up. Expected to be contacted but two weeks has elapsed and you've heard nothing. Don't really mix with villagers so told old friend who works for local rag; was not aware he'd pass it on so will be suspicious of anyone you don't know. You haven't been to the police as you don't get on with them – hint at past incidents involving poaching.

Allow your story to be brought out gradually but try not to volunteer too much too quickly.

Information on the 'Big House'
Old Manor House allowed to run down by previous owners. Used to be open to villagers – Fête, employment, kids played in grounds etc. Recently sold but no one knows who bought it – they've never been seen. New owners have re-built wall – too high to see over – barbed wire on top. NO contact with village – locals sacked, no mail, no milk. Uniformed guards on gate keep everyone away. Noises at night and unmarked lorries go in at night from time to time.

2   The Traitor

This can be a complete lesson in itself, or could form the basis for further development. It could be used to introduce discussion of the concepts of loyalty and trust – for example I have used it as a way of thinking about these concepts with a fourth year class before reading *Macbeth*.

There are two key strategies here – teacher-in-role, and the use of a 'ritual' to build belief, gain commitment, and encourage all pupils to take part. The teacher role is very much as controller of events, and does not require acting skills, merely the willingness to maintain a serious tone and set an example of elevated, ritualistic language.

Background

Give pupils the following information:

Since the defeat of the Dragonlords in the Time of Queen Ria, our country has enjoyed peace and prosperity. Recently however, rumours have been spreading from the North that the various barbarian tribes have banded together and are turning their attention to our country. Acting on advice the Queen or King (i.e. you) has summoned all of her/his retainers to an important council meeting in the War Chamber. No such summons has been issued for twenty years – some of the people will remember the Dragon Wars (and may have fought in them), but some will only know of them through stories and legends.

Getting started: a pair exercise to build role

Explain to pupils that they are to be these people – retainers, warriors, advisers. (You could try to elicit the range of possible people, but point out that any role is open to *any* sex – there's no reason why a girl cannot be a fearsome warrior – and try to keep roles appropriate to context.) Ask them to think briefly about who they are, their status, experience, etc.

Remind them that it's twenty years since a summons has been issued – and it's to the *War* Chamber . . .! 'I wonder what each of you might be thinking about as you make your way to the council meeting – half-rumours, a chance to meet old friends again, maybe a little annoyed at having to leave your own affairs . . .?'

Ask pupils to work in pairs: 'in pairs, as if you are the person you have chosen, talk to each other about . . . Well, whatever you would talk about on your way to this meeting . . .'

Allow a few minutes for conversations to develop, and before they dry up stop the work and ask a few pairs to share – by recounting out of role – the kinds of things they talked about. (They are not to repeat the exercise in role for an audience – merely to summarise the key issues and feelings aired in the pair exercise.)

Gaining commitment: giving pupils some choices

Ask the class how this meeting might take place. What does the room look like? What furniture is there? How will people be arranged? How will they come in? Where is the Monarch? Try to establish a framework for how the council meeting might begin.

Explain that *you will be in role as well* – as the Monarch (ask pupils for suitable name!). Will you be present when they arrive, or will you enter after them? Will there be any sort of formal opening ceremony? Who will manage it? Concentrate only on the details needed to *start*.

Into action

Using whatever the pupils decide in discussion, set up an area in the room and identify where exits and entrances are (chairs can mark them). Ask pupils to enter in whatever manner they have agreed, and to take up positions. (You will either be there, or make an entrance into the space now, depending on what has previously been decided.)

After any agreed opening words, launch into the council meeting by improvising round the following:

'My friends, it gladdens my heart that you have all come at such short notice. In these black times it is indeed reassuring to know I can count on each of you [*look round*] but this is not a time to renew old friendships or rekindle memories . . . I have news of great import which will affect us all . . . (go on to fill in some details of the barbarian threat – elaborate on details of activities heard of or witnessed).

. . . and so I have summoned you all to help defend our country, as some of you have in the past. We thought that with the defeat of the Dragon Lords we could live in peace – but the shadows of evil still are abroad in dark corners, and again threaten our existence. Before we begin our council let us renew the bond of loyalty between us all, in the way we have not done these twenty years past . . .'

Break: organisation

Your serious tone and vocabulary will have signalled the kind of formal, ritualistic mood of the session, and the sense of ritual will have been started when pupils made decisions about the organisation and structure of the council meeting.

Ask what they think is meant by 'bond of loyalty' – how might it be shown? What might people say and do to prove their loyalty?

You have two choices, depending on the confidence of the class and how much pressure you want to put on them:

– establish a common set of words (oath of allegiance, promise, etc.) which each of them will ritually repeat to you

– allow each pupil to word an individual promise, loyalty bond, and say whatever they feel is right and important.

Having established this, decide with the class how this loyalty-swearing will take place (e.g. will each one come forward in a special way? Enter from a common position? Does the Monarch have a special gesture, signal, ritual opening, etc?).

Back into action: deepening commitment

Arrange the space and re-establish positions as they were previously. Signal that you are back in role by adopting the same tone you spoke in before: 'Let each of you approach and speak . . .'

Signal the first pupil to approach – allow her to speak, be supportive and don't worry if she fumbles for words – it *is* stressful – I know, I've been an oath taker. Before the pupil departs, say something supportive that recognises that pupil individually and shows you value her commitment. (This works on two levels: new relationship in role and new relationship as people outside the drama.) Comments like: 'I thank you for your words' or 'You always gave assistance when asked. I thank you' would suffice.

If possible try and find something slightly different to say to each pupil – be creative – value her mother's wisdom, trust in the strength of her sword, remember a time she was the only one who heard the wild boars approach, be pleased to see the daughter again, now a woman . . . and look each pupil firmly in the eye with a calm face.

This ritual will take a long time but it can be very powerful in unlocking feelings – the in-role pressures and tensions at this council are fed by the out-of-role real pressures and tensions in the room. It is vital to get this to work by being totally committed yourself – if necessary stop the drama if tension is too great, or even offer out-of-role asides – 'it's not easy for us is it?' You may well be faced with giggles if your class are not used to this way of working. Some of the giggles will mask nervousness and confusion, so be willing to stop and tackle this in supportive terms – 'To do this properly, we need to respect each other and try not to laugh'. If the pupil in front of you dries up or giggles, allow them space to recover and start again. Accept even a word from them (provided it's genuine).

Allow each pupil to approach, speak, be spoken to and return to their place.

Raising the tension

Still firmly in role, be silent. Look slowly and deliberately around faces, pausing on some. Allow at least a minute of silence (which can feel forever) while you look at them . . . then say something like:

'You have all sworn your allegiance. But words are only sounds . . . Who knows what is in the heart . . .? [*Pause, look slowly and deliberately around, resting on individuals as you continue.*] But someone here has not spoken their heart . . . [*Pause*].

. . . someone . . . and this I know . . . Someone here in this room, is a *traitor* . . .!'

Pause . . . allow a little time for your words to sink in . . . then break the drama and signal to relax and gather on chairs to think about what's happened.

Reflection

Talk over with the pupils how they felt during the ritual and your announcement. Allow talk in and out of role: let them verbalize what they were internalising. You could move to more philosophical considerations by wondering why someone would say what she didn't mean. Discussions can continue to be around and inside the drama, as the drama experience and the out–of–role experience connect.

Continuing . . .?

It is appropriate at this point to harness feelings while they are fresh, and draw on the experience of the drama to shape and deepen a piece of personal writing. Writing will allow pupils space to try to order and make sense of the experience – and I have read some very powerful and evocative work arising from such experiences. Ask pupils to recount the events and their feelings in role – the kind of writing (narrative, poem, descriptive paragraph, etc) can be left to them or may be guided by you.

This lesson can be used to stimulate talk and thence a piece of writing, or could be continued. Further developments might centre on identifying the traitor. An example of how this type of lesson was integrated into a literature-based project is documented in Chapter 9 *A Wizard of Earthsea*.

I have used versions of this lesson to meet a variety of purposes and needs – as part of an exploration of the fantasy genre culminating in the planning and writing of a mini-novel; to encourage reflection after reading *The White Mountains* – where the ritual was important to address a lack of involvement (documented in Chapter 7); to run parallel to the reading of *Dragon-Slayer*; as an introduction to

Macbeth; and even with an 'A' level class studying *King Lear*. All that needs to be done is to frame the background to suit the purpose, need or context of the particular work in hand.

3 The Mystery Document

This session is designed to develop comprehension and reading skills through speculation about, and analysis of, a piece of text – which can be narrative, poetic, factual, or diary depending on the context of the overall scheme of work being followed. Pupils are encouraged to use their reading and comprehension skills of inference, deduction, interpretation, prediction and hypothesising as they reassemble and try to understand fragments of a text, and then to test their ideas with others who have other pieces of text from the same source, while speculating about intention, style and context.

The pupil role is that of 'experts' to whom the teacher-in-role turns for advice and help. As archivists, historians, researchers or museum assistants their interpretations and hypotheses must be rooted in the actual text, but the teacher is not suggesting there is a correct solution – a piece of text may well be interpreted in several differing (and equally valid) ways.

The example which follows uses six extracts from *A Question of Courage* by Marjorie Darke as the stimulus material. Although they can stand as source material in their own right, in this case a second set of aims was also achieved – my third year class were shortly to be using this novel as their class reader and I wanted to set the scene, raise some questions and stimulate their interest before we embarked on any reading. The novel is set at the time of the Suffragette Movement and follows two women, from different backgrounds, who become caught up in the cause. The notion of studying parts of the text, divorced from their narrative framework, could be a useful way of exploring what the pupils knew (if anything) about the historical period, and would help set the context and create a need to find out more about the background and history, which would be valuable when reading began.

As well as stimulating interest, raising questions and promoting reading skills, I also wanted to encourage the class to be more aware of style, audience and intention. I hoped that hypothesising about material they knew nothing about would help them towards a more rewarding discussion of the narrative style of the novel when the pieces were rediscovered in context.

I chose the following extracts from the novel to try to suit all these purposes:

1   In spite of herself she yelled out; begging for mercy, but there was no escape. The tube pressed down her throat into her stomach

with a burning tearing sensation that stretched to the end of her breastbone. She stared up with wide anguished eyes and saw the doctor raise the funnel end and pour a brownish liquid into it.

She must suffocate! Her distended stomach heaved. Pain tore throat and nose, searing tender membrane. There was thunder in her head and a waterfall in her ears. No more . . . no more . . . no more . . . But the pain increased in ferocity as the tube was withdrawn, as if a hand were wrenching out the back of her nose and throat. Her body in revolt, she retched, spraying herself and her captors with vomit.

2   And now they were waiting, one minute . . . two . . . Perhaps Annie had been arrested before ever getting here. Perhaps an accident . . .

The heavy blue curtain behind Mary and Louise slowly looped up and a frail skeleton of a woman with large blue eyes sunk in smudged hollows above cheekbones sculptured by hunger and pain, stepped slowly forward. The impact on the audience was enormous. They roared their appreciation for this heroine who time after time had braved hunger, thirst and torture for the sake of the Cause. Emily cheered with them, tears pouring down her cheeks. For of them all her heart went out to this mill girl, a working woman like herself.

3   A charity performance in aid of 'Distressed Gentlewomen' was today's disguise for the W.S.P.U. meeting. Mrs Pankhurst was to have been there, but she had not yet recovered from the awful battering she had received at the Glasgow meeting back in March. Emily still shuddered at the recollection. The cruelty and bloodshed of it lived on in her nightmares. A sick satisfaction came with the sly memory of wielding her bodyguard's club with drastic effect. She had left a good few bruises back in Glasgow and had been lucky to escape arrest. There had been a lull since then with so many leaders ill, in prison or fled from the country. She had not even had contact with Louise, except for a brief note from Peter telling her . . .

4   Four burly men were making their way down the aisle either side. The men and women seated beside Louise turned on her, snatching the banner. Officials closed in, pushing along the row, treading on toes. There was no escape, but still she went on speaking:

'. . . as the world looks on. It is the shame of England that half its population should be treated thus, denied the privilege as are convicts, and . . .' Her part was done. Half dragged, unresisting, the cloak torn from her shoulders, Louise was hurried into the aisle and ejected from the Hall.

But the speech was not over.

'Convicts and lunatics,' boomed a voice with the power of a foghorn. 'Is this the mark of a mature and well-tried civilization, or will in years to come the finger of scorn and derision be pointed at . . .'

Fury seething and wrestling with her unstable stomach, Emily watched the horsy woman roughly shoved from the body of the Hall.

5   Birds must feel like this. Oh, it was wonderful . . . wonderful! Worth all the scrimping. Lunches of bread and lard. Doing without, if Mam was short, because she wouldn't spare even a ha'penny for the treat of a fresh cob or a bag of chitterlings. Faster and faster! The bicycle whirred; feet flying; created wind shaping the thick folds of her skirt round legs and thighs. Summer Hill Terrace came to meet her and the nerves of her stomach tightened. It was steep, very steep; parallel with Sandpits where the trams ran, a sharp bend at the bottom.

6   There must be an end to this day! Minutes stretching like elastic, making weeks out of every second. It wouldn't be so bad if there was a clock, but there was nothing to go by except the low sunlight thinning through Birmingham smoke, which spread warm patches across her back and on to the workroom floor. Another week or two and they would be working by gaslight. Never mind that! It was today that mattered, this wonderful day, so achingly long . . .

The doorbell tinkled distantly from down the stairs, smothered by the rhythmical whirr of the treadle sewing machine. One of the girls stitching giggled over a whispered remark. The bell sounded with greater insistence. Mrs Harris, red-faced and perspiring, emerged from the privacy of the fitting-room, a pincushion on her wrist like a small hedgehog.

(Each group, in this situation, would receive a different section of text to work on, before sharing ideas collectively as a class and looking for common threads – but there are times, depending on the work's purpose, when each group would have the same piece of text to analyse. The approach is sufficiently flexible to meet a number of needs, but does require some careful preparation.)

I copied each extract, in spidery handwriting, onto plain paper, and 'aged' each piece (by covering the paper with tea, drying it quickly in a hot oven, and charring the borders to lose the straight edges).

Each piece was then carefully torn into seven or eight fragments. I removed one fragment from each extract, and added it to another of the sets. The fragments of each section (minus one piece, and plus a surplus piece) were then placed in an envelope, and labelled

'Property of Leicestershire County Council: Documentary Archives Ref. A' (or B, C, etc.).

Each group was to be presented with a set of fragments, and their tasks would fall into several stages:

(a) Assemble fragments.
(b) Read and copy out section.
(c) Try to tease out what information could be gleaned – literally and by inference.
(d) Consider extra fragment, speculate on missing piece (and negotiate with other groups?).
(e) Hypothesise and speculate about the piece. The working framework was as follows:

1   Teacher to explain that class are to be historians, researchers, archivists who work for local museum. What kind of things would they do in their jobs? Then explain they have been invited to a meeting to advise on and consider a recent find; they will be in groups.

2   Teacher goes into role as Head of Urban Development with local council – greet and thank experts for giving up precious time to come and help with a problem. Quickly set the scene . . . Some recent demolition work unearthed some very old-looking papers which appear to be interesting, possibly unique value (?) . . . Can they help you to identify and understand these papers . . . in role, stress you don't know anything . . . *They* are the experts . . . and the papers are so old and brittle they crumbled into pieces so that you cannot read them . . . You have been recommended to consult the museum as they have dealt with this kind of thing before.

Any questions? Then proceed to give out one envelope to each group.

3   Break drama, out of role check if context and roles are clear. Explain or discuss possible stages for examining the documents – assemble, read, etc.

4   Back in role, ask each group to handle the fragments very, very carefully and ask them to see what sense can be made of them . . .

5   Allow a lengthy period for groups to piece their fragments together, decipher them and begin to speculate about the assembled version. Go round the groups to offer support in role – encourage deeper analysis by probes such as I wonder who might have written this and why? . . . What does this bit mean? . . . What on earth is that about? . . . Have you any idea what those initials stand for? . . . I wonder what it was written for? . . . What makes you think that? . . . etc. The teacher role will be impressed by the experts' skills and yet also, as teacher, be able to press, through role, for deeper reflection.

25

6   Reconvene large meeting and ask each group to share their version, ideas, views, speculations, questions, theories. If groups did not exchange surplus fragments in the previous phase it may well happen here naturally, as each group reads its assembled extract.

7   After each group has reported, and ideas begin to emerge, consider the extracts as a whole group . . . 'Are they separate or one 'thing'? . . . What is it (are they) about? . . . Which bits don't we understand? . . . What questions have we raised? . . . How might we find out some answers? . . . Do the pieces link? . . . What sort of style are they written in? . . . What does this then suggest about why they were written or who might have written them? . . . Are there common threads? . . . Is there any sequence? . . . Is it all here? . . . What's missing? . . . etc.

8   Draw the session to a close by asking what should be done now. Is it possible to write a press release – several national papers have made enquiries (pupils could actually write this press release).

In the particular example of the extracts I used from *A Question of Courage* the class actually spent a following lesson finding out what W.S.P.U. was, and researched the Suffragette Movement. A colleague came in (in role as visiting expert on this period) and gave an illustrated talk, and pupils tried to see what new light was cast upon the extracts now that these new background facts were available. I then introduced the novel and said it dealt with the same period . . . and the opening paragraph was one of the extracts . . . This was interesting since no one had suggested it was a 'story" and raised all sorts of questions about narrative styles and conventions.

I have used variations of this framework in a number of ways as a way-in to *Z for Zachariah* (and consideration of diary style and conventions) – as a prelude to studying Chaucer with an A level group (this was especially fascinating as they grappled with the unfamiliar language and style and tried to interpret it) – as part of a project on the Great Fire of London (using extracts from Pepys's diary and facsimiles of real documents) and, in a joint project with the humanities department, an exploration of the Luddites, again using facsimiles of documents from the period as a starting point.

In each case the pupils are engaged in making meaning from text and deepening their perceptions of style, audience and intention by focusing upon language. Individual meanings take form through the building of shared meaning, in a way that allows *all* to contribute. The immediacy of a concrete stimulus and the 'as if' authenticity of the tasks provoke curiosity, inquiry and speculation, and it is through talk, in a variety of modes, that meanings are developed, sharpened, tested and elaborated. It is pupils' interpretations, based upon their scrutiny of the evidence in front of them, which receive status and credence from the teacher role – the teacher does not have all the answers!

Although some careful preparation is required, the fragments will remain as a future resource within the department, and it is a good collaborative exercise to plan, select and prepare materials with colleagues.

4 'Haunt-Away – the ultimate experience!'

This was the proclamation on a poster produced by a group of second years, as an attention-grabber for their bus company's new venture – a mini-break visiting 'haunted' locations.

The half-term project used drama to provide a context in which pupils, in role as employees of a local bus company, had to create and research a commercial scheme, deal with organisational problems, persuade local people to support the scheme, and ultimately to try to convince their board of directors not to axe the scheme! It involved talking and writing in styles appropriate to different audiences and shaping work according to perceived intentions – factual, descriptive, persuasive. I chose to exploit the 'as–if' drama mode as talking, listening, reading and writing in role mean absorbing, assimilating, interpreting and communicating with a different perspective. The work was based on the pupils' own experiences and their understanding of others, but given meaning and purpose through the real, yet not real, vehicle of drama.

My starting point was the idea of a local bus company organising mini-breaks (prompted by a leaflet delivered through my door), but I decided that the actual choice of tour-type would be theirs – which would give them a sense of ownership and control. My framework would act as a possible map through the work – and following it would be equally feasible whatever the theme (supernatural, sport, etc.) chosen, provided that it was made clear in role, this is what the bus company had decided!

In order for the latter stages of the project to involve the pupils fully, I considered it important that they felt the work was 'theirs' – the mini-break had to *matter* to them . . . and I also wanted the opening sessions to have the potential for making them aware of outside pressures and external forces in the background . . .

Getting started

I gave out the memo shown on page 31, and asked them to read it as if they were employees of the Greyhound Coach Company who had received the memo on their desks when they arrived for work this morning. Would they understand anything from it other than the setting of a task? I decided to use the written memo rather than

English Through Drama

GENERATING & SEQUENCING IDEAS — A FRAMEWORK

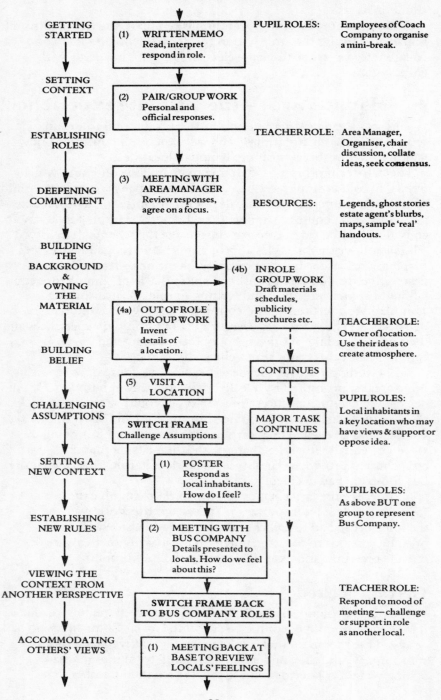

28

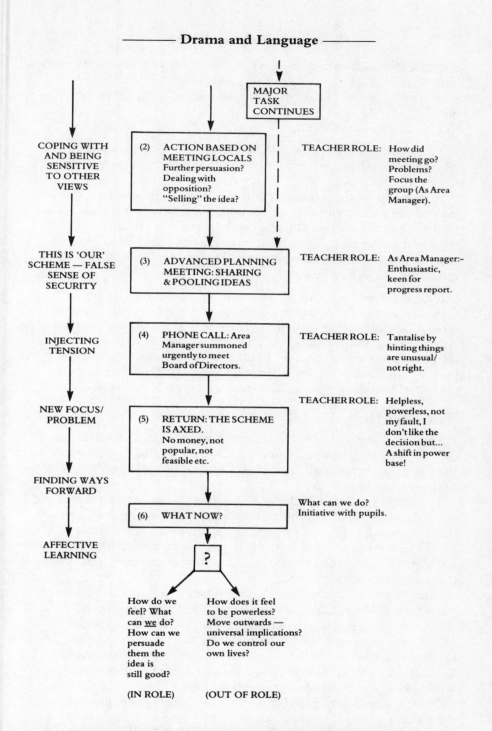

MAJOR
TASK
CONTINUES

COPING WITH
AND BEING
SENSITIVE
TO OTHER
VIEWS

(2) ACTION BASED ON
MEETING LOCALS
Further persuasion?
Dealing with
opposition?
"Selling" the idea?

TEACHER ROLE: How did
meeting go?
Problems?
Focus the
group (As Area
Manager).

THIS IS 'OUR'
SCHEME — FALSE
SENSE OF
SECURITY

(3) ADVANCED PLANNING
MEETING: SHARING
& POOLING IDEAS

TEACHER ROLE: As Area Manager:-
Enthusiastic,
keen for
progress report.

INJECTING
TENSION

(4) PHONE CALL: Area
Manager summoned
urgently to meet
Board of Directors.

TEACHER ROLE: Tantalise by
hinting things
are unusual/
not right.

NEW FOCUS/
PROBLEM

(5) RETURN: THE SCHEME
IS AXED.
No money, not
popular, not
feasible etc.

TEACHER ROLE: Helpless,
powerless, not
my fault, I
don't like the
decision but...
A shift in power
base!

FINDING WAYS
FORWARD

(6) WHAT NOW?

What can we do?
Initiative with pupils.

AFFECTIVE
LEARNING

?

How do we
feel? What
can we do?
How can we
persuade
them the
idea is
still good?

(IN ROLE)

How does it feel
to be powerless?
Move outwards —
universal implications?
Do we control our
own lives?

(OUT OF ROLE)

(MAJOR TASK OF PRODUCING PUBLICITY MATERIALS, POSTERS, BROCHURE,
SCHEDULES, ETC. CONTINUES PARALLEL TO DRAMA.)

throwing the idea straight out in a meeting as I wanted to move them into the drama slowly and gradually, with time to think. They also would have a sense of role and purpose when they came to the meeting . . .

Two activities followed:

1 In pairs, as employees who had received the memo, pupils talked informally over lunch or coffee about the memo and their responses.

2 I then asked the pupils to get into groups of four or five, gave each group a title from the memo, and asked each group to select a section head, who would be responsible for the work and organisation of the section. Each section head was then to chair an informal section meeting where initial thoughts, feelings, ideas, questions, etc. could be aired . . .

(Only one group seemed concerned, in these meetings, about the financial state of the company. The suggestions I eavesdropped on were imaginative, but sometimes over-ambitious or just impractical. Circulating as unobtrusively as possible, I was able to pick up on things like this which pointed to the role the area manager would play: I would need to refer to finances and to competition and my role would set the context and introduce a note of reality.)

The meeting

I explained I was going to take the role of area manager and arranged the pupils in a circle, seated on chairs. I had a small desk (as part of the circle), and explained that when I was sat behind that desk talking to them I was in role.

The meeting started with my welcoming everyone, hoping they'd had a chance to read and think about yesterday's memo, and stating that this was the only item on today's agenda – all other business would be temporarily shelved. I stressed urgency, importance, secrecy because of competition etc. and then threw the meeting open for comments and suggestions.

What followed was a lively session where we explored a range of possibilities. My role allowed me to welcome and accept each suggestion and then throw it back for consideration . . . Could we afford such an operation? Could we fit that all into a long-weekend? Do you think people will go for it? What do the rest of you think? This allowed me to channel the discussion into practical and workable schemes, to answer questions about finance and redundancy with worried comments like, I don't really know . . . if the scheme works it won't come to that . . . we need a sure-fire money spinner that people will enjoy and tell their friends about . . . and to gauge interest in various alternatives. I listed final suggestions

**GREYHOUND
Coach Services**

GREYHOUND COACH SERVICES

INTERNAL MEMO   CONFIDENTIAL   DATE: Thursday

TO: The following Departments and Sections:
       Publicity; Public Relations; Schedules
       & Routes; Customer Services; Market
       Research; Development Think Tank; Costings.

FROM: Area Manager - South - Western Group

As you are all aware, we have been facing considerable
losses recently.   Our local services continue to run
at a very narrow profit margin, and fierce competition
has made our position more difficult.   We need to
maintain a good service to the community and therefore
must seek new ways of increasing profits which could
make up for many of the loss-making services, e.g.
in rural areas, in order to avoid redundancies and
cuts in services.

We have had considerable success with our Day Tripper
excursions, but rival firms are still undercutting us
on the most popular routes.   The company is now
considering the idea of long weekend packages - mini-
breaks with accommodation, meals and guided tours of
places worth visiting.   A small coach could, we hope,
take a group of mini-break customers to interesting
places with everything laid on.

Could you give the idea your urgent consideration -
tomorrow's meeting in my office will place this item
first on the agenda.   Any suggestions, ideas,
practical problems etc., you raise at the meeting
will be more than welcome.

Can I also stress that, at the moment, this suggestion
must be kept confidential within the relevant sections
and departments - we don't want someone beating us
to it !

David Eckes.
AREA MANAGER

and asked them which we should investigate as having most
potential. We quickly settled on the idea (coming up several times in
various forms) of a long-weekend visiting 'Haunted Houses' – and
even managed a provisional name for the mini-break – 'Haunt-
Away'. The preliminary exercises had certainly made the talk at this
meeting purposeful and allowed time for absorption of the idea.

We listed a number of areas for urgent consideration: customer
needs; market research; how to sell the idea; research on likely
locations; the number of locations possible to visit; timings; facilities
needed; accommodation – any night visits/haunted hotels? Then I
asked each section to go away and make some practical suggestions
around the questions we had formulated.

Building the background

In the next session, when each section met to consider their next
move in more detail, I, as teacher, gave out to groups copies of local
legends, books on ghosts and hauntings, and some estate agents'
blurbs (I had spent the previous evening visiting up-market agencies
collecting property details of country houses, pubs, vicarages,
cottages, shops – anything with an interesting picture!)

I asked each group, as themselves, to take one of the locations, and
using the resource material and their own imaginations, to build a
background for this location as a haunted building: name, type of
haunting, local stories, sightings, history, anything, in fact, that
would be useful to the bus company. An individual written
assignment which grew out of this was for each pupil to produce a
description of one location (not the one the group had chosen) – and
to write the section on it that appeared in the 'Haunted Places in
Britain Gazetteer'. (Subsequently we had this typed and bound and
illustrated.)

Working on tasks in role

We had a brief meeting again where each section presented a location
to the whole group, and we discussed the pros and cons of each and
tried to categorise them and find some variety in locations to make a
range of experiences available over the mini-break.

Each group then went away, still in role, to begin thrashing out
material and concrete proposals for the scheme – posters, booklets,
hand-outs, schedules, itinerary, maps, guides, etc. Each group had
to use *other groups'* locations as well as their own, and also to do some
market research which involved surveys and questionnaires.

This promised to be an organisational nightmare, but I was soon
able to relax and let the pupils find their own directions. I didn't have
to itemise what each group had to produce, but was able to advise (in

role as area manager) on any problems or lack of direction. In practice we blurred in and out of roles all the time.

I began to show them that it wouldn't be a straightforward planning task by asking them to deal with the owner of one of their locations who might not be pleased at the prospect of 25 people traipsing round her property. Once again, I led up to this by a simple pair exercise. In pairs one pupil was an employee of Greyhound Coaches, and one was the owner or her representative. The Greyhound Coach person was to telephone the owner, explain the scheme and try to fix up an appointment to visit her at the location.

The work during the pair exercises was sharpened by reconvening the meeting and asking for the responses people had found . . . what were people's reactions? I had gently to keep them in role during this, and didn't ask every pair to report.

I then asked which location we should visit first, and for some details about it.

Visiting a location

I used a mobile board, wrote the name of the house on it, and drew a door-knocker. I explained that I would also be in role, and told the class the board was the front door. Would they start when ready . . . pause – finally one small knot of pupils approached the door and knocked. I ignored it! They knocked again – no response. Mutters from the class – 'didn't you tell them what time?'; 'might be deaf'; 'I'm sure someone's in . . . .' Finally I opened the door (by moving the board) and peered through this imaginary small opening saying, 'Go away, I'm not interested in anything today!' before shutting the door again. Confusion, uncertainty . . .

I broke the drama to briefly discuss the situation out of role . . . what will you do now? Why did he do that? . . . They decided to write a note and post it . . . This time the door opened and I said 'well, why didn't you say so . . . oh . . . what a lot of you . . . you didn't say there would be this number . . .' and we were into the drama again. They had to negotiate entry with this old man, try to gloss over his rudeness and explain what they were about patiently and carefully as he kept mis-hearing them. Finally they got a conducted tour. During the tour the old man was slowly drawn into recounting history and showing off locations – 'This is where she walks . . . you know she's here 'cos it goes terrible cold all of a sudden . . .' (I used all the details pupils had previously invented, and the role brought their stories to life.) They then left, thanking him.

(I had toyed with taking a more challenging role as recalcitrant caretaker who knows nothing of the arranged visit and is quite obstructive, but decided instead that building an atmosphere was the most vital function of this role.)

Taking a different perspective

In order to help them see other viewpoints and explore various attitudes to the scheme – the effects on *people* (positive and negative) – I decided to switch the pupils' roles at this point to being the local villagers. The lesson started as I showed a poster that had appeared in the local village Post Office. This asked interested villagers to meet with Greyhound Coaches to hear about a scheme which would involve the village being part of an organised coach tour of haunted places.

I asked one section to prepare to address this meeting and deal with any questions from the villagers. While they prepared themselves, I talked over with the rest of the class what local reaction might be: 'What might you feel . . . What would you want to know? . . . Do you believe in the stories? . . . Do you want to be famous? . . . How might the village be affected? . . . Could you cope with all the day-trippers? . . . Might it bring new jobs? . . . What about peace and quiet? . . .'

The meeting

The exploratory discussion (with its deliberate emphasis on *you*, not *them*) had indicated quite a negative feeling about the proposal so I decided that in role as a local I would support it! I would also ask the representatives from Greyhound Coaches questions to challenge them or to support them, depending on the mood of the meeting.

The meeting started slowly, as villagers listened patiently to the plans, until one girl said 'But I don't want hordes of people standing staring at me or my house.' From then on things got lively and the Coach Company representatives had to work hard to win support.

I found my role becoming focused in firstly trying to elicit as much information as possible from the Greyhound Coach representatives while being sympathetic, and secondly trying to present a positive side to the villagers – business, jobs, etc. However, I also took quite a quizzical stand and supported my opponents (friends!) by saying, 'Ah I hadn't thought of that . . . but would the problem be that bad?'

In order to stop the meeting degenerating and losing its spontaneity and passion, I broke the drama and posed the question 'I wonder what these people thought about as they went home?' and then asked each pupil to say quickly, in role, what was in her mind. This provided a concentrated focus which summarised the range of feelings.

The general feeling of unease, doubt or even hostility was still prevalent. How would they now cope with viewing the problem having seen another perspective?

Final preparations

Running simultaneously with this drama was the work, in role, of each section to produce brochures, materials, plans, drafts etc. for the 'Haunt-Away' venture. Now seemed a good time to bring everyone together to share each section's work so far (and comment on it), and talk about dealing with the villagers.

The section who had addressed the meeting reported back, indicating the strength of feeling against us. There was no satisfactory way of resolving it (suggestions included travel concessions, a 'face-lift' for the village, and the offer of part-time employment) and I wasn't sure whether the locals would have had much power anyway.

As bus company employees, they were quite sensitised to the feelings and worries of the locals, were very willing to find ways to accommodate them, and were quick to home in on potential supporters in the village who might win over others.

This was quite a lengthy session, and much of the sharing had to be held over.

The axe falls

During the following session of sharing progress to date I had a phone (as a visible symbol) on my desk. The criticisms of each groups' work so far were very supportive and constructive and the questioning highlighted new lines of development. I decided to let *each* group report their progress as the process was proving valuable (both orally and for each group's product), and only interrupted the session with the telephone call during the latter stages of the final report.

I decided (for time reasons only: the lesson only had 7 minutes left to run), not to leave them but instead tried to make clear my own surprise at this decision: 'But we're well on with all the planning . . . I know but . . . yes but . . . surely we can talk more about this . . . oh . . . so the Board have all agreed . . . yes . . . I see . . . well of course I'm sorry . . . yes . . . I see . . . well I've got everyone here, I'll tell them now.'

There was visible tension in the room during this phone call: though the actual content of the news could only be surmised as they tried to interpret my comments, they all sensed it was serious and directly concerned them!

When I broke the news of the scrapping of the project there was stunned disbelief and righteous indignation. I had to endure the brunt of all this . . . but I was as powerless as them . . . and indicated the major reasons seemed to be lack of confidence in the scheme and uncertainty about financial success.

The lesson ended with a quick reflection out of role about what these people would, or could, do now, and about how they felt.

What now?

The class decided to try and take it further and asked if it was possible to meet the directors. I indicated I would try my best but first we would have to get our act together and appoint spokespeople. The major part of the lesson was given over to formulating a case to be presented – what grounds would we argue on . . . what could we *show* . . . could we demonstrate it would be successful . . . had we anything concrete to take along . . . how would we enthuse and persuade the directors?

Facing the board

Three colleagues agreed (after much grovelling on my part) to act as the Board of Directors and we arranged a meeting, after I had briefed them on the events so far. All the class attended the meeting, but had chosen five representatives actually to argue the case. They presented a coherent, glowing description, and dealt with a truculent and narrow minded director very sympathetically and persuasively. The pièce de résistance came when they invited the board and their families to try out the scheme in a 'dry run'. The idea was that the board, having seen it work and enjoyed themselves would agree . . . and in fact the board agreed to defer the final decision until after this trial run.

Looking back

We never really had time (bad organisation on my part) to explore in depth issues arising from the project, but the excitement and enthusiasm generated a very high standard of written work; the 'as-if' context had deepened their commitment and sense of involvement, and enriched the talking, listening, reading and writing processes by making them purposeful and important to the pupils. Most notably, we had created a climate whereby the sense of audience was real enough to encourage clearer and deeper thinking about style, tone and presentation through a focus that made these processes explicit.

In this instance I deliberately let the pupils choose the actual subject, but it would have been equally legitimate to have decided this in advance – the framework is sufficiently open ended. All that is needed is for the area manager to say that there is a scheme for mini-breaks on ____ and the early discussion can still be on general lines but with a more specific focus.

3

Pulling Out the Threads . . .

In all English Language teaching the basic task is to enrich and extend children's experience of language, both spoken and written, and to provide a constantly expanding variety of opportunities to use spoken and written language in real and imagined situations. Children will draw on everyday language (including home dialects and mother tongues) for these purposes, as well as on the growing range of language registers and varieties of which they are becoming aware.

NATE *evidence to the Kingman Commission*

Strategies used in the four language projects

The structures, frameworks and strategies for employing drama as an integral part of the processes that take place in an English classroom have this concept at their core. Drama offers the opportunity to use language in a variety of situations and allows a fusion of thinking and feeling which is given form and articulated through language (both spoken and written). Language development takes place not through linear predetermined steps or phases, but as the pupils, in their roles, interact with other roles and the context. This process of language development can be represented diagrammatically as shown below.

Language Development

New context created
↓
New roles established and built
↓
New relationships developed
↓
New language demands made to
suit context and roles
↓
Interaction: language demands tackled
↓
Reflection – raising into consciousness
the language demands and responses
↓
Language development

(I have to thank the Wakefield Literature and Learning Project for the basis of this framework.) In this model of language development, pupils actively explore ways to use language, starting from where they are and their intuitive grasp of language, and moving to a more conscious, deliberate awareness of language.

The previous chapter introduced in practical ways some key strategies to aid this process. The strategies are used in a variety of forms, and adapted to suit differing and specific purposes within the overall context of language development. Later chapters offer more examples of introducing and working with these strategies, but the four examples I have given so far illustrate the four modes that constantly intermesh:

- *Teacher-in-role* used to set the scene (The H.D. Factor); to move quickly and easily into the drama (Haunt-Away); to create tension (Haunt-Away, Mystery Document); to provide a model of language use (The Traitor); to organise group roles and tasks within a common context (Mystery Document); to build pupil roles, belief and commitment (all four projects) and to place the onus and responsibility for making decisions and directing the work on the pupils (Haunt-Away).

- *Whole class drama* is often the major organising form (The Traitor) as the opportunities for interaction, involvement and a range of participation are present.

- *Pair exercises* can help build pupil roles (The H.D. Factor) and allow pupils space to develop their own role and clarify their own perspective (The Traitor). Pair work also offers pupils a secure, non-threatening way to formulate and develop their responses to a context, issue or other roles (Haunt-Away).

- *Small group work* often takes place within the larger whole class context (Mystery Document, Haunt-Away) and allows pupils to collaborate and share. In small groups, pupils have opportunities to air their feelings or ideas (Haunt-Away) and to tackle tasks and resolve problems collaboratively.

Significantly talk, both in and out of role, also takes place as the pupils move between the drama and reflection, and it is during reflection (in pairs, small groups, or as a whole class) that learning becomes conscious. *Meetings* are useful ways of exploring a range of attitudes, setting contexts, or reflecting on events (The H.D. Factor, Haunt-Away), and the use of a *ritual* (The Traitor) can be a powerful way to gain commitment, build belief and inject tension. *Written tasks* and non-drama activities grow from and feed the drama context, and the roles and context shape the style, tone and form of the writing – from journalists preparing a draft lead article for their editor (The H.D. Factor) to characters writing their thoughts and feelings, in role, about the accusation that one of them is a traitor (The Traitor). Drama can also provide the leading edge to a scheme of work (Haunt-Away) which covers a whole range of writing tasks, with the 'as-if' context giving the work a purpose and importance. The fundamental aim underpinning all the work is 'to enrich and extend children's experience of language . . . and provide a constantly expanding variety of opportunities'; the strategies described are designed to facilitate this.

Additionally there are three inter-related, and often inter-connected, strategies that are not really exploited in the lessons in the previous chapter, but which I have found immensely valuable in slowing down action, and encouraging deeper thought about the meaning of a particular incident – either within a text or within a drama that is being freshly created. They are secure, non-threatening strategies, and can be used to start a drama, to explore a key moment within an experience, or as a means of encouraging reflection.

The three strategies: *still image*, *soliloquy*, and *hot-seating* are illustrated in context (and action) in following chapters, but need a little explanation and consideration of their potential.

The still image

The 'frozen moment', 'photograph', 'tableau' or 'freeze frame' are interchangeable labels for what I term 'still image'. Essentially, in a still image an individual, group or class freeze themselves into positions at a selected moment in a situation. Every detail becomes significant and conveys layers of meaning. Facial expression, body position, positioning within the group and scene and movement or stillness combine so that attention is focused upon what the image is trying to communicate (and what it actually communicates) and how it does so. The participants have to consider very carefully what they want the image to say and mean; observers can discuss what they 'read' into this image. Attitudes, feelings, relationships, implications can all be discussed by the class; each group will need to consider very carefully how they think a character would feel, or how they (in role) feel. It is a very powerful way of focusing attention on a specific moment within a text.

Recently I was working with a colleague on *Lord of the Flies* with a very difficult, boisterous all male fifth year class. We wanted them to imagine how Ralph and Piggy feel at the moment when Ralph has seen a ship and realises the signal fire is out. This was to be a prelude to exploring and understanding what happens when Ralph and Jack confront each other on the mountain top (the class had not quite reached this point in their reading). We asked the class to imagine we were Ralph and Piggy, and to sculpt us into a still image, frozen at the moment Ralph turns to look up at the mountain. The following dialogue accompanied the exercise:

Teacher: What would be going on in Piggy's mind?

Pupil One: What the hell's going on!

Teacher: How can we actually make him look like he is Piggy saying that?

Pupil Two: Squinting ['*Piggy*' *tries – laughter*]

Teacher: Anything else?

Pupil Three: Shock

Pupil Four: He ought to have his mouth open ['*Piggy*' *tries, laughter, but not disruptive of the process*]

Teacher: Anything about how Piggy is standing, or arm movements . . .?

Pupil Five: He'd be sitting down.

Pupil Two: He's probably looking round to see what was happening.

Teacher: Do you want Piggy standing or sitting?

Chorus: Sitting

Pupil Six: On the floor ['*Piggy*' *takes up position*]

Teacher: O.K. – That's Piggy and what he might be thinking, what about Ralph? What do you want to show?

Pupil Two: I think when he thinks the fire's not in he'd be mad. [*Teachers as Ralph and Piggy take up positions*]

Teacher (Piggy): Is Piggy frightened?

Chorus: No

Teacher (Piggy): Has he seen there's no smoke?

Chorus: No

Pupil Seven: It's Ralph thats seen it . . .

Pupil Two: And Piggy wonders what's going on . . .

Teacher (Piggy): So I'm squinting and sort of gormless. [*Laughter – one comment is – like usual miss! – but not nasty.*]

Teacher: So Piggy is bewildered, incredulous, squinting, not really sure what's happening, and Ralph is angry because he's realised . . . shall we try? . . . one, two, three. Freeze! [*Laughter, but boys very involved in observing image!*]

Teacher: Is this O.K.?

Pupil Eight: That's all right [*sounds appreciative*].

Pupil One: Yeah.

Pupil Two: I think Piggy looks, well, too comfortable, he looks at ease like [*demonstrates relaxed position*].

Pupil Five: Lean forward . . . [*Cross talking as 'Piggy' is directed into a position they are satisfied with.*]

Teacher: Freeze! [*Pause as class assimilate image*] . . . I wonder what Ralph and Piggy are thinking about?

Not only did the boys have to consider the practical problem of making the image look and feel right, but they began to move into the minds of those two characters at that moment. They were both inside and outside the experience, as the above transcript demonstrates, and used their own initiative both to shape and interpret the image. This 'demonstration' provided the group with a secure base and clear understanding of what was expected when they were asked to make their own still images (from the mountain top scene) and it began the process of helping them to empathise with the characters. (A full account of this lesson, and how the strategy was used appears in Chapter 6.)

Because the still image is a precise, controlled, slow and thoughtful activity, it provides a form for pupils to give concrete shape to their views of a situation or theme, creates opportunity for reflection, and allows for implications to be teased out by discussing what can be 'seen' in it and by experimenting with subtle alterations to it. An abstract discussion of a theme or characters, in a novel for example, can be sharpened by creating a still image which tries to communicate something about the theme or feelings of the characters or the relationships between them.

The still image is also a very effective way of starting the drama, or re-starting action. By focusing on a particular moment, and asking the pupils to take up positions and think themselves into the situation before the action starts, you have an excellent 'control' device, which allows the pupils to move into action or interaction from a definite starting point. To help create the atmosphere, build the situation and help the pupils think themselves into the moment, a very useful strategy is to use 'teacher-narration' as a way of setting the scene, or recreating the atmosphere.

As a preliminary to reading *Lord of the Flies* I wanted a class to explore an analogous situation – they were to be 'themselves' (i.e. fourth years) who were suddenly stranded on a mountain top. The teacher had gone to look for help and had not returned. They had to cope, organise themselves and make arrangements for passing at least one night on their own. The first session had finished as they had settled down for the night in a hut, and they had written down their feelings in the last 10 minutes of the session. The second session needed to recreate that moment. (In real time it took place two days after the first.) I asked the group to recreate the still image of that moment at the end of the traumatic (but exciting for some) day and then close their eyes. I re-evoked the atmosphere and feelings of the end of the first session by reading from pieces of work they had written in role.

'I'm cold . . . I think it's going to be quite an experience . . . I wish I'd never come on this trip . . . I wish I was in a warm bed at home . . . hope I don't start sleep walking . . . I'm scared stiff, I wish it was warmer . . . I hope someone comes soon, I wish this was a dream and I could pinch myself and wake up . . . I need support from people . . . even though I'm surrounded by people I feel lonely . . . this isn't how I thought it would end up . . .'

I then moved the action on by narrating the scene that would greet them as they woke . . . 'the fire has gone out – which was no one's fault . . . there is a cold grey light coming through the window . . . it's bitterly cold . . . when I clap my hands I want you to wake up and bring the scene to life . . .'

One final point: the still image is easily accessible to both pupils and teachers wary of the term 'drama'! It is controlled, requires only an ordinary classroom, does not expose pupils to the fear of 'acting', slows down energetic pupils who want action, channels their energy into a precise and structured frame, and requires pupils to collaborate, share, and make and communicate meaning.

Soliloquy

This can be used to add an extra dimension to the still image. It requires pupils to engage directly with the character, role or situation, thus helping them to sharpen their own perception, and allows the rest of the group access to the inner mind of the character which can then be discussed. It can provide an effective way of enabling the pupils to contribute individually to the collective atmosphere, or it may provide insights and opportunities for reflection and discussion on characters and their motivations.

There are several ways of organising this access to a person's mind: the teacher may touch a participant in the still image on the head or shoulder and ask her to speak aloud her thoughts in role; another pupil can touch a character he wants more information from; or a pupil can place his hand on the character's shoulder and speak the thoughts for her. Each method will highlight different things.

In the first session on *Lord of the Flies* (referred to previously) the still image had been used to focus on a key moment. The pupils were stranded on a mountain, and their teacher had just left to see if he could get help. In order to help build the atmosphere, and help them build belief in the situation I asked them to freeze, then speak aloud their thoughts. Some of the replies were illuminating:

> 'I'm really cold – I've got little food left. I'm scared.'
> 'Ooh! – I can't wait!'
> 'I'm scared – why has he left us on our own?'
> 'I just want to go back home.'
> 'I'm not panicky, I just want to know what's going on.'
> 'I'm not bothered – I'm glad he's gone!'

Coming straight after the teacher-in-role's announcement and departure this provided a focus for the action, gave an opportunity for the drama to slow down so that the implications of the situation could begin to be absorbed, clarified a range of feelings, gave pupils an initial, individual starting reference for themselves and directly helped them engage with the piece of writing they were to do at the end of the session.

In a different session on *Lord of the Flies*, the pupils in role as the boys on the island had just witnessed Jack's challenge for leadership and his storming off when the boys did not support him (a decision *they* made, incidentally). The scene was then frozen and I placed a hand on individual boys' shoulders, asking them to answer in role why they had voted, or not voted, for Jack when he had challenged Ralph. Among the responses were:

'I want to be rescued, where he doesn't care.'
'He's strong and I like him more.'
'Because Ralph's doing all right.'
'I'd like to be one of his hunters, and he'd do well.'
'Ralph's a sensible leader.'

This initiated a lively discussion on why the boys don't vote for Jack and yet later desert Ralph, and prepared the way for future group role play (discussing their reactions in role) and future writing (in role).

Hot-seating

In some ways this strategy is very similar to the soliloquy. The difference mainly lies in the fact that the soliloquy is used when the pupils are inside the drama experience, whereas in 'hot-seating' a character or role can be removed from the context of the situation and questioned by pupils who are not necessarily in role themselves. This gives the pupils the opportunity to challenge, question or test assumptions about a character within a novel or play and to move to a deeper understanding of that character.

If one is using this device to explore character motivation with a novel, it is sometimes better to let another teacher (or yourself) be the role or character who is questioned – especially in the early stages of such work – since the questions are likely to be very demanding both in the sense of textual accuracy and in interpretation – though the danger is of course that the teacher can easily provide or model her answers to fit in with her own interpretation. However, it can begin to open out for pupils their understanding of a character if the teacher responds sensitively rather than dogmatically. Allowing a pupil to become the character who is hot-seated will place heavy responsibility on her but, with supportive questioning and discussion by the group on the answers offered, the pupils will be given opportunity to test their own responses and reactions.

If two pupils undergo the process simultaneously, both being the same character being questioned or challenged by different groups in different parts of the room, or if pupils take it in turns to answer questions in the way they feel the character would have done, then this will press the class into awareness of the variety of interpretations a character or the text will bear, and will encourage the pupils to present and justify their opinions. These opinions and assumptions can then be tested out at further stages in the story to see if any modification of interpretation is required, or if any shift in understanding has taken place. Mr Evans in *Carrie's War* by Nina Bawden is an example of a character who is perceived in differing ways as the novel progresses, and hot-seating Mr Evans at various stages in the story would help the class to be aware of this.

It is sometimes helpful to relieve the burden of responsibility placed upon a pupil being hot-seated by allowing two or three pupils collectively to represent a character – so that they have mutual support in deciding how to answer the questions – a device I term 'corporate character'. The class may also take on a role so that the hot-seating process takes place within the drama. This can sometimes give their questioning a more definite purpose and focus upon a key area.

Examples of hot-seating appear in the documented accounts of actual lessons. At the end of a session on *Lord of the Flies* it was obvious the majority of the pupils saw Ralph as a 'bore', and a 'spoilsport'. In order to help them realise Ralph's point of view, I started the second session in role as Ralph before the assembly, and the boys were able to question me directly, outside the drama and the book, about my feelings and reasons for calling the assembly.

Their questions were on the lines of:

'You've had all day to call the assembly.'
'Why do you call it now?'

'We were having a good time up there, why'd you spoil it for us?'
'We was only having a little dance y'know.'

The ensuing discussion prepared the ground for an exploration of
the assembly which Ralph called, and his reasons for calling it.
(A full account of this lesson appears in Chapter 6.)

During the second session of work on *The White Mountains* by
John Christopher, described in Chapter 7, three pupils were a
'corporate character' being questioned by members of the
Community Council, as to the truth of his story, his trustworthiness, his value to the community, what new information he
had brought, how he found them, etc. This required a grasp of the
main events in the story and an accurate recall of them, and meant the
pupils were empathising and identifying with the character and the
situation, and drawing upon their own abilities to explain, to
convince, to inform, to persuade and to justify.

4

Drama and the Novel

*I think I understand the story better because just sitting down
reading a book isn't very interesting, but sitting down
talking about it and dramaring it learned me more about the
characters and how they felt. It makes you want to be there
to make the difference.*

Fifth Year Pupil

Rationale

Reading a book is an active process – we are conscious not of the
words but of meanings made. When our pupils read books there may
be no observable outcome (unless we consciously seek to determine
the response) apart from some sort of introspective recall. The
imaginative participation that we feel as readers is almost a sort of
armchair acting, an internalised drama, as we recreate for ourselves
something which approximates to the author's original conception –
we become, to borrow an idea from Tolkien, sub-creators of a
secondary world. Often a book which is read a second or third time
can be viewed in a different way from on that first reading – yet the
actual words have not changed, only the interpretation, or meanings,
of those words. The words then are not as important as how we
respond to and use the words – how we fit them into our own
framework of experience. As the Bullock report says: 'to read
intelligently is to read responsively; it is to ask questions of the text
and use one's own framework of experience in interpreting it. In
working his way through a book the reader imports, projects,
anticipates and speculates on alternative outcomes . . .'

The class novel is still a powerful and effective learning medium,
where the experience shared amongst a group allows a joint response
to enrich individual response; our pupils share the individual
experiences which they bring to the reading and contribute to the
experiences they take from it. This process is very akin to the drama
process.

Much drama work lays stress on feeling – one feels one's way into
the person and into the situation. The problem is how to lay equal
stress on thinking, on understanding people and situations so that the
pupils do not just play themselves and resort to the clichés and
stereotypes that can characterise 'free drama' work. Conversely one
criticism of English Literature teaching is the way pupils
intellectualise emotions – Gavin Bolton cites the example of pupils
who can explain how Lady Macbeth felt on receiving Macbeth's

letter, or who can write a summary of it, but they do not actually *know* how she felt, meaning the pupil has not had access to the affective experience. By bringing together the drama experience and the reading experience, pupils are given access to felt and intellectualised experience, with each feeding the other in the creation of a personal response.

Too often a fusing of drama and literature is seen in terms of re-enacting the story, a semi-theatrical representation of the text. Rather than ask pupils to re-enact a scene, the drama process should have the more subtle role of enabling the pupils to explore what lies underneath a scene – at a level which allows them to apply their own embedded knowledge and experiences. Often dramatic moments will hinge upon issues rather than scenes. If events become of paramount importance, or tied to a predetermined narrative line (i.e. the plot of the novel) then there can be no true exploration. The drama process offers participants the opportunity to 'dwell in the moment' (to borrow Byron's phrase), so that the story becomes the framework inside which a deeper exploration of a character's feelings, motivations, fears or beliefs can be laid open, and a situation can be viewed in terms of past decisions and future implications.

Drama can make a unique contribution to the study of literature: English is concerned with knowledge at a stage before it can be expressed, literature is the conscious application of this knowledge in action; and drama is an important and valuable means of enabling this knowledge to become conscious. Role-play can deepen engagement with a work of fiction and allow a pupil to explore and make her own meanings – to become what David Jackson terms an 'active meaning maker'. Interaction with a book brings about meaning; in drama pupils create a personal understanding of the novel which is shared within a group experience, open to challenge and modification, and thus deepened. This understanding may be factual, intellectual or affective, as the drama establishes connections between the reading experience and the pupil's own experiences. When a work of fiction is the pivot for talking, writing and drama activities, then we provide models of language ranges, expand and clarify the language experiences of our pupils, encourage articulation of understanding and help pupils make connections between what they already understand and any further knowledge the work of fiction opens up.

Drama can be used at any stage of reading a class novel – before, during and after – each with its own focus.

Activities before reading can stimulate a desire to read the text, arouse curiosity about the situation or pose questions on the theme or subject matter. The overall aim will be to prepare pupils for the experiences of the book in ways which will enable them to make connections between their own lives and the lives and experiences of characters in the novel, or to make an unfamiliar context accessible.

Activities whilst reading is in progress will often focus on key sections of the novel. The aim will be to combine existing textual knowledge (retention of events, incidents and understanding of character and context) with personal experience in order to predict and analyse in an affective mode the outcomes of decisions and actions. Through role play, the experience of the situation and the feelings of the characters become personalised.

Activities after the book has been read will allow the teacher to discover responses to the book, and possibly to challenge these responses so that there is full interplay between the novel, individual response and shared response.

The following chapters take each of these stages and consider these aims and possibilities in more detail by illustrating practical ways of working with texts before, during and after reading.

Firstly, however, I wish to distinguish two distinct ways of using the drama process within each stage, each with its own aims (though in practice the two complement each other). I term these approaches *direct drama* and *indirect drama*.

Direct drama

The *direct drama approach* is rooted firmly in the characters and situations of the book. It is an approach that should help pupils to understand more clearly some of the ways in which an author constructs a plot and deals with the various choices of plot and characterisation that have to be made. This approach does *not* require the acting out of scenes from the book, but it may involve the reconstruction of scenes so that pupils can suggest modifications and interpretations and compare these to what the author actually did. By tackling a specific section or incident in the novel and exploring it – by becoming the characters and experiencing their motivations and choices in the light of what has been picked up from the reading so far – pupils can do this.

For example, in some sessions on 'Lord of the Flies' the pupils took on the roles of boys on the island, sometimes the key characters, sometimes only partially sketched characters, and the emphasis of the work was upon the struggle for leadership between Ralph and Jack, symbolising the struggle between rules, order and sense and freedom and anarchy. In order to understand each boy's feelings and thoughts, pupils role-played situations that actually occurred in the novel (e.g. Jack's challenge to Ralph), and situations *around* those key moments (e.g. boys discussing their feelings about Ralph when he stops the dance and calls an assembly on the mountain top); and they compared what they made happen with what Golding makes happen. The pupils began to move more deeply into the text and the characters – to understand them by becoming them, as opposed to being told about them or analysing them objectively.

Indirect drama

The *indirect drama approach* makes use of analogy, rather than the story or the characters from the book, in order to allow pupils to experience the 'feel' of the book, or to explore themes in the book as they affect their own lives. Analogy uses feelings, not facts, and enables pupils to build their own metaphor in order to unlock the metaphor of the book. (A process Dorothy Heathcote calls code-cracking.)

To use *Lord of the Flies* again, before reading the novel I wanted to lay down some reference points which would enable the pupils to personalise their understanding of Ralph's conflicts as leader by connecting them with their own experiences. This was done in two stages – firstly as a class of fourth year pupils they had to appoint a spokesperson and reach a consensus decision about a motion to present to the School Council; and in later sessions they become pupils who were stranded, without adults, on an Alpine holiday, having to fend for themselves. When reflecting on the novel they recalled vividly their drama experiences – they were able to appreciate Piggy's situation by recalling and realising that the person who makes proposals must be someone they respect as a person before his ideas are respected (one boy's contributions to the drama had been steadfastly ignored), and when discussing leadership they drew on their experiences to sharpen their understanding of Ralph's dilemma – 'Janice was feeling that as everyone voted for her she *had* to do it – even though she didn't want to', 'if you've got a teacher or adult organising you they're sort of higher up, but when it's your mate you don't really take no notice of them.'; 'Janice wasn't the same person when she was voted in . . . she was above us . . . and wasn't with us anymore, she was sort of separate'.

Analogy, rooted in their own experiences which they bring to a drama, enables pupils to establish their own connections with a character or theme.

Planning work on a text – *Carrie's War* – Nina Bawden

I shall now consider the questions of where, how and why to use drama to enhance responsive reading of a work in relation to an actual text. What do I want the class to explore? What will my focus be? How will I get started? Is it better to work in 'direct' drama or through analogy? What strategies would help? Do I need to create a context prior to reading? Are there some key moments we could spend time considering in depth? These are some of the crucial questions to be thought through when planning drama work in and around a novel.

Let us apply these questions to *Carrie's War* by Nina Bawden – a book which raises a multitude of issues.

What might be worth exploring?

My initial list was as follows:

- evacuation – who, where, why, effects and the experience. Historical background/context for the novel
- coping with a different way of life and expectations – would analogy help? Cultural differences?
- families, and relationships – old/young; brother/sister; parent/child
- loyalty and disloyalty – conflicting loyalties
- judging people on first impressions – sympathy switch – people are not always what they seem
- conforming to cultural expectations and norms
- coping with eccentricity
- attitudes to mental handicap
- consequences of rash actions and judgements
- the supernatural
- nothing stays the same

I could have carried on, but already had more than enough.

Finding a focus and mapping options

I opted for a safe, conventional way in, and decided that an understanding of evacuation, from both perspectives (evacuee and host) would be very helpful in both setting the context and in keying into the early experiences of the book. Having chosen the focus, I had to then put together a framework for it. Because I wanted to raise awareness of the two perspectives, the pupils' roles were really decided for me – they would have to *be* evacuees, but at some point we would have to switch roles and prepare to *receive* evacuees. I wanted the drama to create a shared experience to set alongside Carrie's early experiences – so the drama work was to take place *before* any reading of the actual text.

I had two choices now – either to plunge in and deal with the historical context of the evacuation and World War II as it arose *in the drama,* or else to find a way of setting the historical and social context in a way that would not burden pupils with facts, but engage their interest and provoke their curiosity. I mapped these options in the following chart.

Be Evacuees (1941)
↓
Set situation by going straight into role as a teacher giving information to class about final preparations for the evacuation.
↓
The implications for them of this – family scenes.
↓
How do they feel about being uprooted?
↓
Do they understand why they are to be evacuated?
→ *Feeding with facts.*

Be Modern Day Historians
↓
Prepare a museum exhibit? Analyse, review info, facts, accounts to make a 'presentation' – T.V. programme?
↓
Possible context: Exhibition about life for ordinary people and children in World War II.
↙   ↘

Authentic research e.g. Interview relatives – Local Record Office – Newspaper Archives.

'As if' research e.g. interview me in role – Sharing research with class in role.

↓
Exhibition
↙   ↘

Authentic display, documents, artefacts.

'As if' – still-images, 'Pathe-news' clips – diaries/ documents.

Though I was attracted by the 'distance' role, I felt that the experience of *being* evacuees would create more of a need to know within the drama, and would allow for engagement at a feeling level. It seemed to me that understanding and articulation were likely to be significantly richer as a result of the emotional investment, and as the group were used to working in these ways with me there would be no need for the less-threatening strategy of distancing them (which with another group, less used to role-play and teacher-in-role, could have been more appropriate).

Planning a framework

I wanted to get them 'into' the drama quickly, with the minimum of preliminaries, so decided to use teacher-in-role to set the context and sketch the background, and then to pause to see what they had assimilated of the situation, before returning to consider the implications in role. In the early stages of the lesson we would switch in and out of drama; the out-of-role reflection would enable me to assess when, and what kind of, factual background needed injecting.

The framework I devised was this:

1   Teacher-in-role announcement to set context and move us into drama quickly and economically without long explanations. Teacher role – class teacher, pupil roles – class about to be evacuated. Distribute letter about final arrangements, check everyone understands where to meet etc.

$$\downarrow$$

(May be necessary to break drama early on, to check what pupils have inferred about roles and context.)

2   Explain letter must be taken home (use actual archive material?) – discuss implications in role, teacher to answer queries, fears, etc. but role is 'middle status' – unable to change decision!

$$\downarrow$$

3   At home scenes – children bring letters home (pair work – mother or father – 'have you see this letter our Edie has brought home . . .?'). Resource material (*actual* documents, papers, evacuation orders etc) needed to give authenticity. Liaise with History Department? Emphasis upon understanding why, historical context and thence to personal family responses.

$$\downarrow$$

4   What does it mean to us? Still images, soliloquy – family members or groups as children depart for station. (Photographs useful resource here.) What will we take? Prized personal possession – what special thing will you take?
    ★Write a letter from *parent* about you (the child) – which will be sent on to potential hosts.

Switch frame to consider from new perspective

1   Village meeting. Teacher in role as Government Official

wanting hosts for evacuated children. Give out leaflet (again find original archive material). Will you take them on?

↓

2   Pair work – villagers discussing idea of taking in an evacuee. Are they willing? What are their worries? What problems might arise?

↓

3   Meeting – giving out letters from parents and allocating children who are about to arrive. Organisational problems. *Tension* – the children should have been here an hour ago and we are still not ready. Pair exercise – 'how I have chosen and prepared for this child?' *New tension* – Teacher in role as villager opposed to idea and full of hearsay and stereotyped images of scruffy urchins, thieving brats etc.

This framework would have enabled several key things to happen: it was a safe model, it set the background, it led directly into the opening section of the book, it would help empathy with the early situation Carrie was in, it required looking at the same experience from differing perspectives, and it necessitated some factual input.
   However, what I really wanted was something which would go deeper and help the pupils be *inside* the experiences of the novel. Though the events were rooted in the historical fact of the evacuation, to me the book was about universal issues. This framework didn't seem to lay a base from which to make the universal connections, and I was worried we might get caught up in the narrative drive (what happens next) and lose the parallels between the drama experiences and the reading of the novel. On one level the book is 'about' evacuation, but it was also about so much more that this framework wouldn't tap into. As the class were quite experienced in role-play, I felt we could try something more adventurous and potentially risky.
   Returning to my original list of issues, there seemed to be some which would be within the children's own experiences. By drawing on their own experiences of loyalty and disloyalty, of forming judgements on people and of obeying authority, they would have a resource to bring to the creation of the shared drama experience; the experiences they would draw upon might not be conscious, and I wanted to use drama to help them make this knowledge more conscious – the process Bullock described as 'what is known must in fact be brought to life afresh in every knower by his own efforts'.
   I therefore decided to work directly from experience, by asking them to be themselves (a third year class) in a contemporary setting analogous to that of the World War II evacuation. I wanted to try and

make my role that of an intermediary caught in the middle between unseen authority and the children, which would be analogous to the Mr Evans ⟷ Aunty Lou ⟷ Carrie situation.

An alternative framework

The situation or context had to have the following factors:
(i)   Away from home ⟶ sudden, do they understand why?
(ii) They will have to conform to someone else's expectations.
(iii) There is no show of compassion for them.
(iv) Being 'soft' is not on.
(v)   There is another way to view this authoritarian 'control'.
I had to find a context that would facilitate these, yet be accessible. Brainstorming gave rise to the possibilities mapped below.

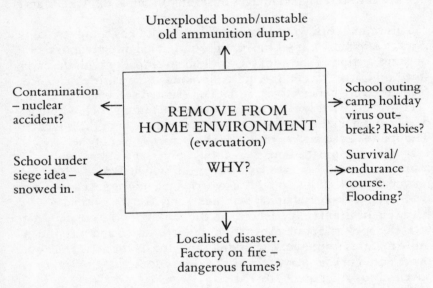

Unexploded bomb/unstable old ammunition dump.

Contamination – nuclear accident?

School outing camp holiday virus outbreak? Rabies?

REMOVE FROM HOME ENVIRONMENT (evacuation)

WHY?

School under siege idea – snowed in.

Survival/ endurance course. Flooding?

Localised disaster. Factory on fire – dangerous fumes?

Whatever I chose had to necessitate the wholesale sudden removal of a large group of children because their lives could be in danger. I also wanted to avoid a context which would necessitate considering other issues – Chernobyl-type disasters or contexts which involved political or moral issues would only blur the focus.

Ideally, I should have liked to explore this choice of context with the pupils, but I opted for teacher agenda and structure (hoping that I would have room for manoeuvre) since in this case a lengthy negotiation process would lose the impact I wanted to create. The new framework I devised only covered the first session: I would need to plan again after I had assessed what was happening and decided what purposes the drama would need to serve in future sessions.

The plan

1   Teacher in role – straight into drama. 'Please follow me now, gather your coats and bags, don't argue, just follow me quickly – I haven't time to explain yet but you need to be somewhere safe. Did anyone hear the news this morning? Well it's to do with the rabies scare – now just follow me.'

2   Break – how do you feel? What's in your mind? 'You are herded onto a coach; while travelling you hear the following news item on the radio' (play tape – localised severe rabies outbreak, all movement restricted, children being kept together and sent to various centres, many parents at work out of area and won't be allowed to return, army to deal with potential animal carriers, a person is dead and six more in isolation with suspected rabies).

Soliloquy – thoughts as you hear this. (Teacher role – coach driver – knows nothing, just following instructions if interaction happens here.)

3   Arrival at large house. Teacher in role welcomes pupils to 'Downlands' – large, imposing house. (Photo?) Ushers them in – friendly but harassed – emphasis on 'being quiet please' – polite but seems worried by their arrival. Registration, name collecting, form-filling details. Soliloquy/frozen image?

Group work – discussing what's happened, impressions of this person, fears, worries etc.

4   Teacher role introduces unseen authority presence 'it may not be what you're used to but we'd better get things straight and right from the start – I am the housekeeper (or butler) and you will be in my charge but remember this is Mr Smith's house and he has strong views on things' (elaborate to hint at possible conflict between unseen presence and teacher role – uneasy tension?).

Teacher role reads list of rules and regulations – quite restrictive-leading to question and answer session based on this – teacher role to support and try and explain why these are necessary – sympathetic to any query, but has to support the rules 'this is Mr Smith's house'.

5   Break drama, *out of role* create plan of house, facilities and

environment. Which bits are 'off limits' (referred to in previous rules?), sleeping areas, arrangements for daytime activities.

$$\downarrow$$

6   Back in role, teacher extends list of regulations (drawing on plan created by pupils) – emphasises quiet, orderly movement, off limits areas, expectations of behaviour.

Group work: sharing impressions of the place so far, 'how are we going to get on here?'

$$\downarrow$$

7   Interrupt group work: in role announcement 'there's too much noise (veiled threat) – Mr Smith insists you are quiet at *all* times' – sympathise with pupil view but powerless to alter Smith's views!

$$\downarrow$$

8   Out of role – how could we approach and talk to Mr Smith? Can we rely on housekeeper for support? How do we think she feels about us? Our situation? Mr Smith?

If possible try to find a way to talk to Mr Smith – in role 'rehearse' this.

★*Written task*: A diary entry or letter home describing the day and responses to it – anything that pupils want to say to parents is fine!

Some Development Possibilities
● Depending on content of letters, confront pupils in role with the fact they are giving a distorted view – ungrateful (if this emerges in written work). How would they feel about private thoughts being read? What if housekeeper role warns them 'he's reading your letters' first?
● Open discussion – 'where should the drama go now?' Opportunity for pupils to negotiate and control directions.
● Meeting/talking to Mr Smith.

Both frameworks are equally valid, with different foci within the overall purpose of keying pupils into the experiences and characters of the novel, and in particular creating a shared experience to bring to and set alongside the early experiences of the book. What is important is to be quite clear about the learning areas that will be opened up by the choice of approach. Having identified what areas you feel worth concentrating on, you then have to find a context and roles to suit the purpose, and have in mind strategies that will help meet this purpose and build the røles. I have found frameworks and flow charts a useful way of planning – remembering it is important to be flexible and respond to situations as they arise!

5

Ways - in

Activities before reading a text

Strategies and approaches

Many secondary school pupils are quite apathetic about embarking on the shared reading of a class novel. Drama can provide an active way to provoke curiosity or arouse interest and challenge ideas.

A simple, yet effective way of arousing interest is to begin to tell the class the story, asking them to tell you the point at which they think the story is getting really interesting (in itself an intriguing area). At that point you can muse . . . 'I wonder what happens next? . . .' and you have the basis for short group improvisations which will encourage discussion and reflection on narrative choices and options, and will also furnish you with rich opportunity to see and hear pupils' perceptions of narrative.

A straightforward way of introducing the text is to set up a pair or small-group improvisation around a theme or personality in the story. This can make connections between pupils' own experiences and the experiences in the story. For example, pair work involving a family argument about boyfriends or girlfriends that parents disapprove of, developing into talk about dislike or distrust of people from different family backgrounds (with the pupils suggesting what the clash of culture/belief is), could begin some work on *Across the Barricades*.

A simple pair or group exercise of this sort need not occupy a great chunk of the lesson and can begin to move the pupils toward an understanding of a central point, or allow them to explore a relationship which can act as a reference point when the novel itself is started. (An example of this strategy is detailed below.)

Improvisation and role play around an analogous situation, environment or theme to that of the book will also lay down reference points, rooted in experience, for future discussion of key moments or concepts. The lessons described on page 49 are of this kind. Before reading *Lord of the Flies* I had the class involved in a situation where they had to appoint a leader and spokesperson who then had to organise the class and arrange for a majority decision to be reached. In subsequent reading of the novel, I was able to use this experience to move the class towards an awareness of connections between their own lives and experiences and the experiences of the novel. The lesson developed into a situation where pupils were stranded, without any adults, in a bare hut on the Alps. In subsequent reading of the book we called upon their experiences of decision-making and trying to cope on their own. They could see direct connections and thus understand from an affective (as well as intellectual) base Ralph's predicament, inner conflicts and problems.

A variation of this pre-reading activity is to shift the frame the pupils are operating within so that they are both inside and outside the experience of the book. A very useful strategy here (already described in the preparation for reading *A Question of Courage* in Chapter 2) is to use mock documents which relate directly or indirectly to the text or context of the novel and cast the pupils in role as historians, archeologists, anthropologists or archivists who have to interpret the documents, make deductions, draw inferences and formulate hypotheses.

A very famous Dorothy Heathcote lesson illustrates this process, when, before reading *The Mayor of Casterbridge* she passed out copies of Henchard's Will:

> *Michael Henchard's Will*
> *That Elizabeth-Jane Farfrae be not told of my death or made to grieve for me,*
> *and that I be not buried in unconsecrated ground,*
> *and that no sexton be asked to toll the bell,*
> *and that nobody is wished to see my dead body,*
> *and that no mourners walk behind me at my funeral,*
> *and that no flowers be planted on my grave,*
> *and that no man remember me.*
> *To this I put my name.*
> *Michael Henchard*

In searching for information necessary to understand what made Henchard feel compelled to write this, not only do the pupils begin to make preliminary assumptions about the character and his motivation (which they can refer to and modify when reading the book) but also they will be curious about the situation, raise questions that need answering, and be willing to have a crack at an apparently weighty tome!

Alternatively, you could ask the pupils, as historians or museum curators to build an exhibit around the period and area, using still images, drawings or symbolic representations (and therefore requiring research). You can be the sponsor who then asks for a conducted tour.

It is important to identify and be clear about the specific purpose you want the drama to serve – for example when working with *A Wizard of Earthsea* (described in full in Chapter 9) I wanted to tackle the resistance previous classes had exhibited to the setting, and the difficult language. The two examples which I am about to give had very different purposes, and the drama strategies and lesson frameworks illustrate this. The work on *Of Mice and Men* builds from pair exercises and is rooted firmly in a situation directly parallel to that of the characters in the book; the lessons on *Frankenstein's Aunt* were designed to be part of a thematic approach to a literature text and could even exist independently!

The important questions to address are: What can be offered through drama which will give pupils an experience against which to weigh the experiences of the book? What do I need to do to help the pupils get inside the experience of this novel? What are the problems – unfamiliar context? Difficult language? Length? Narrative construction? Going beyond the immediacy of the story?

Of Mice and Men – **John Steinbeck**

I wanted an experience which students would be able to draw upon when thinking about the characters of Lennie and George, and the relationship between them. Beginning to understand the characters, their relationship and the pressures upon them, through articulating and reflecting on a felt experience, would make an immediate connection.

The framework is tightly controlled and uses role-play exercises. What is important are the discussion and reflection that take place as people's feelings become articulated and we begin to think about the two characters; that is, *the post role-play discussion is crucial to tease out implications, issues and feelings*, which can subsequently be set against our understanding of Lennie and George in the novel.

1 Ask pupils to work in pairs, and decide who will be A, and who will be B. Explain that A is quick, lively and copes easily with situations. B however is the opposite, doesn't pick things up easily, doesn't find it easy to understand difficult or complicated things, is a bit 'slow'. Explain you want them to do a simple task together – without being silly or 'acting'. Choose a simple everyday task and do it together, by mime, movement, sound, dialogue, etc.

2 Allow a few minutes for this to develop. If some pairs are indulging in over-the-top stereotyping you will need tactfully to point this out – the 'slow' one is *not* necessarily physically or mentally defective!

3 Break the exercise, and add a new dimension. A and B have a bond that keeps them together – each pair are to decide *what* this bond is (e.g. a family tie). The bond between them is sufficiently strong to keep them together. When they have decided this ask them to work on their task together again.

4 Allow this to develop then bring the class together (sitting in a circle) to discuss what was happening. Was there any difference in the relationship and way of working together in stages 1 and 3?

What? Why? How was it shown? How did A feel? How did A treat B? Consider the range from different pairs. What about B? How did B feel? How does B feel about A? Why? Tease out implications of feelings that may range from compassion to frustration, anger or confusion. How are these feelings shown? Are any feelings hidden? What? How are they hidden? Why?

5 A and B are now going to try and get a job together (they always work together). Allow the pairs a few moments to decide what this job might be, then ask them, in their roles, to talk together about how they will handle the employer, what they will say, who will speak, etc. A may have to prepare or brief B – and they may have past experiences which point the way for how to handle this. Allow this to develop.

6 Ask for a pair to volunteer to be 'interviewed' about this job. This pair will interact with you in role as their prospective employer, while the class watch. In role you can make this interview as tricky as you feel the pair can cope with – does B speak for herself? Why not? Try and get questions past A to B! Be willing to accept A but you will need reassuring about B!

7 Discuss with the class the ways A and B responded and reacted, and why this was so. How do A and B feel about each other?

8 Ask the pairs now to be working on the 'job' they applied for. Ask the A's to go and start, and gather the B's to you. Quietly brief them that they have done something wrong and have to tell their partner (A) about it – and allow this situation to develop.

9 Discuss, out of role, how the A's responded and the ways B's told their partners!

10 Ask for another pair to volunteer to work on their task, this time you will be a fellow worker and will join in with them whilst the class watch and listen.

Allow the activity to start then join in. In role be rude about B – work-rate, standard of work, challenge A – 'why do you put up with him/her – do you always do her/his talking?' Push this as far as you can to see how A and B respond.

11 Discussion and reflection on the exercise, and the overall situation.

Reading of the story can now begin, and the experiences drawn on and set against the events and experiences of the story.

Frankenstein's Aunt – Allan Rune Pettersson

This is a humorous novel, in which the central character, Hannah Frankenstein, inherits the now dilapidated Castle Frankenstein from her nephew, and returns to the village with hopes of restoring it.

The novel is very accessible and easy to read, and I used drama to link the reading of the novel with all the other activities for half a term. The scheme can stand on its own, but it does make for a coherent approach in which all the elements of English work together within a unified context and where the literature text feeds other activities, and vice versa. There were several key experiences (rumours, hostility, mistrust, misconception based on past experience) that the drama would emphasise in order to deepen the reading of the novel, which can easily be read superficially.

Establishing the Roles and the Context

When the pupils came into the classroom the advertisement shown below was written on the board.

WANTED

HIGHLY SKILLED AND PROFESSIONAL RENOVATORS AND RESTORERS FOR AN EXCITING AND LUCRATIVE OVERSEAS CONTRACT.

LONG TERM COMMITMENT (MINIMUM 3 MONTHS), ALL EXPENSES PAID. MUST BE WILLING AND ABLE TO WORK UNSUPERVISED AND ON OWN INITIATIVE.

APPLY IN PERSON WITH FULL DETAILS OF PREVIOUS PROJECTS WORKED ON TO :—

REVAMP LTD. 01-953 4619.

We discussed the advert, what it seemed to imply (and any difficulties of vocabulary), and what sort of people might apply. We then brainstormed as many different types of trades and crafts that could possibly come under the umbrella term of 'renovation and restoration'.

I then explained that they were renovators and restorers who had responded to the advertisement and convened a meeting in the Revamp offices with me in role as managing director. Having welcomed them, I referred to the advert and checked they were all skilled, experienced, available for work immediately, prepared to work overseas, and able to commit themselves for a minimum period of three months. This was done quickly, and queries answered in very general terms. I explained that before giving details I needed assurance about their expertise – could they please tell me some details of their last project?

I broke the drama at this point and asked the pupils to form small groups – contractors and companies – who were to give themselves a name and invent details of their last job. Having allowed groups time to talk and prepare, we reconvened the meeting.

As each group introduced itself and described its last project, I made notes and checked the range of skills they had needed to employ, asked them what problems they had encountered and was generally impressed and pleased. Names had been carefully chosen and (out of role!) I was really impressed by their descriptions of previous projects for example:

'Mixed Sisters' were a group of very articulate women who had helped restore the stonework at York Minster; 'Aquafire' had refurbished Trafalgar Square Fountain; 'Let There Be Light' were skilled in leaded windows and stained glass.

Having established them in their roles, and allowed each group to build its own identity, I proceeded to give details of the job by reading a letter from the client (which allowed my role to have only the same information as the renovators).

Dear Revamp Ltd.,

I have been given your name by Count Lugosi whose 17th Century mausoleum you contracted to renovate and repair last year. I was very impressed by the tasteful workmanship, decor and furnishings your firm provided, and wondered if you would care to undertake a contract for me? I have recently come into possession of an old dilapidated castle which was left me by my nephew on his death. Unfortunately, the castle is in a state of disrepair and has been extensively damaged by a fire, leaving it exposed to the elements. For the past ten years it has been totally neglected. I should like to renovate and refurbish the castle, returning it to its former glory, but have been unable to recruit a suitable workforce locally; therefore in addition to designs and plans I should like you to recruit the necessary skilled people. I will be willing to remunerate your workforce generously, and can arrange for materials, etc. to be on site when they arrive. Would you please respond as soon as convenient?

Yours sincerely,
Hannah Frankenstein

There was a lively discussion about the job, the letter, and a certain amount of caution – many wondered about the name, the fire, and the apparent problem in recruiting local labour. I was unable to

provide much more information, except that Revamp had accepted
the contract which was in Transylvania, and would make all
arrangements for permits, travel and accommodation. There was
some urgency since I had been let down at the last minute by
previous applicants – but what information did they need or what
questions did they have?

After an intensive questioning session we came out of role, and I
asked groups to draw up plans, proposals, etc. We sketched a floor
plan of the castle on the board together, and invented any details
about layout as a class collaborative exercise.

Building the background

Before the next session pupils, in their role as small firms, used their
rough plans to draw up proposals and designs related to their
particular field of expertise. This involved a lot of research to find
suitable materials and ideas for rough sketches. 'Mixed Sisters'
produced some excellent drawings of gargoyles and stonework
suitable for a Mid–European Gothic Castle, and 'Changing Moods'
really went to town with interior design – collecting details of
tapestries and furniture – even designing fabric samples! Because of
the enthusiasm generated I had to allow considerable time for this
phase of the work; what the drama context had done was provide a
need and an impetus to research and write for a specific purpose.

Setting out

Once the work was well in progress, we picked up the drama focus
again by reconvening a·meeting in the Revamp offices. I outlined the
travel arrangements, explained Miss Frankenstein was very pleased
with their draft proposals and asked them to sign a contract whose
final clause is shown below.

```
    I agree to the conditions specified above, and
    hereby absolve Revamp Ltd. from liability for
    anything that may occur during my contracted
    time of working on Castle Frankenstein.


    Signed_____

    Witnessed_____

    Dated_____
```

This contract had two purposes: to commit the pupils to the drama, and secondly, within the drama itself, to provide a tension. The class queried what they were signing – especially the implications of the last clause (which many of them didn't really understand) – and they were unhappy even when I assured them that this was standard procedure! At one point I sensed they were going to refuse to sign en masse, so merely said 'well of course I can always find other people, and I would be unable to recommend your firms to any future employers'.

This caused resentment, confusion and doubt – but they did sign!

I briefly outlined the travel arrangements, answered any last minute queries, and wished them success.

The remainder of the session was devoted to individuals preparing personal travel documents, passports, work permits, identity cards, tickets and vouchers, as a way of helping to build their belief and deepen their commitment.

The journey

I wanted to move the drama on in the next session so that we could concentrate on arriving – and finding things were not going to run according to plan!

I asked the class to arrange some chairs in the middle of the room to represent the railway carriage, with seating and entrances. The class posed for a group 'photograph' (still image) at the station and each member, in turn, spoke aloud his or her thoughts at that moment, just before boarding the train. I explained that when I clapped my hands they were to bring the photograph to life, board the train and find their seats. When they had settled I then 'froze' the scene again and used teacher narration to move the drama on: 'It has been an exhausting two days, the change of trains in Paris went smoothly and you are now approaching your destination. You are tired, stiff and a little hungry.

It is now past midnight, and there is a terrible thunder and rain storm outside – flashes of lightning illuminate craggy mountain peaks and dense forests. Suddenly, you sense a change in the train's movement . . . you are slowing down and with much clanking and hissing of steam the train shudders to a halt . . . you rub the windows and peer out through the rain. You have arrived . . . (pause) . . . when I clap my hands bring the scene to life . . .'

I allowed a few minutes for the group to play at collecting their bags, stretching, and striking up conversation . . . the more dominant personalities soon began to organise and pose questions to the group . . . and I quickly froze the scene and once again asked several group members to speak aloud what was in their minds. We held the scene whilst I touched individuals on the shoulder (an already established signal) and together we all shared and built the experience of relief, confusion, exhaustion, trepidation and uncertainty.

I had already planned that my role was to be a station–master who would merely impart information and neither offer nor give help; when I sensed the group floundering a little I approached them . . .

Arrival

'Picked a bad night to travel didn't you?' was my opening gambit. In role I was quite unsympathetic and unhelpful, even uninterested . . . no, there were no taxis! No–one has a car here! . . . telephone lines were down due to the storm . . . the village is one mile that way . . . and walked off. Cursing the station–master, Revamp and the world in general, the group trudged off in the direction of the village.

Using still image and teacher narration I quickly narrated their trek along a muddy track to a sprawling collection of wooden houses. One, slightly larger, had 'Taverna' written on the door. Retreating behind my mobile blackboard (with 'Taverna' written on it above a picture of a door-knocker), I asked the group to unfreeze the image and bring the scene to life.

After much persuasion I finally opened the door, and, in role as a God-fearing innkeeper, I berated the group for disturbing my rest at this unearthly hour. I quickly sensed the panic and confusion this role caused and relaxed, making tentative friendly overtures by noticing their wet condition, muddy shoes and heavy bags. With more persuasion I switched the style of the role slowly to give control and security back to the group, and was reluctantly persuaded into letting them in, peering anxiously outside before pointedly bolting and locking the door. I had never heard of them or Revamp, but looked visibly shaken whenever the castle was mentioned. I wouldn't allow myself to be drawn into conversation about the castle, and avoided the issue by changing the subject, pretending not to hear, or looking blank. I was finally persuaded to put them up for the night . . . but would not commit myself to more . . . and I told them they would have to make do . . . I left to try and rustle up some food . . . and to allow the drama to continue for a few moments before stopping it.

Out of role we considered options and aired feelings. I left sufficient time (deliberately planned but not always managed) and they spent the last 20 minutes writing in role their thoughts and feelings as they tried to make themselves comfortable . . . a letter home to a loved one or parent, a diary entry . . .

Further sessions were given over to planning what to do next: contacting and dealing with Revamp, exploring the ruins, communicating with locals and *being* locals talking about the arrivals and speculating on their reasons for being here. We started our reading of the novel and soon established parallels, drawing on the story to provide impetus and focus to future work. As villagers discussing the past history of the castle and their feelings about it being restored, or as restorers trying to win the confidence of these locals, the reading, talking, writing and drama activities were woven in and around our reading of the novel. Issues and characters within the novel were thought about and understood more deeply, and the satirical and fantastic content was found to have more universal implications and connections with pupils' own lives.

6

Challenging Assumptions

Activities whilst reading a text

Strategies and approaches

The main thrust behind drama work whilst a text is being read is to encourage the pupils to make sense of what they have already read and to anticipate and speculate on the next stages. Amongst the aims of the drama will be that of enabling pupils to identify with a character or situation, to articulate their own feelings about this, and to begin to relate the experience to their own lives. It is useful to bring the pupils' own real experiences to bear directly on the imaginative experience of reading the novel, and, through drama, key points or incidents can be explored in a way which is personal and matters to the pupil.

If we take as an example a point in a novel where an important decision needs taking, it is necessary for the pupils to understand why the decision is taken. By exploring the situation in role, considering the alternatives and then implementing a decision, the pupils have the chance to live through the situation both as themselves, and as the characters. Thus when improvising the conflict between Ralph and Jack on the mountain top in *Lord of the Flies* the pupils will bring to bear all their own experiences of conflict and vying for leadership or status, and combine this with what they know of these characters in the novel. There is a fusion between personal experience and the experience of the book which helps pupils to make their own meanings in their reading.

Another key moment for work on a novel is when you wish pupils to explore what they anticipate will happen and set this against what the author decides. The arrival of the Swiss helicopter in *Brother in the Land* by R. Swindells is such an example: if you have created still images and enacted scenes of post-holocaust existence, responses and feelings on sighting the helicopter can be explored through soliloquy and bringing a frozen image to life. Subsequently, if the teacher in role as the Swiss official intervenes (on the lines of the actual narrative) and delivers his ultimatum (using words from the text) and then departs, new feelings and suggestions can be aired. These can then be set against the actual text: the despair, hopelessness, anger and frustration are recognised; the options open to the survivors and the decisions various groups and individuals actually make can be compared with pupils' own feelings and decisions made during the drama.

The purpose of the drama then is to deepen and personalise understanding at both affective and cognitive levels, not to act as a vehicle for play-acting. A superficial enactment of 'exciting' scenes will not achieve this; while pupils should not become overburdened with textual and interpretative accuracy, neither should the opportunity to delve into meanings *behind* the action be missed.

It may be that the teacher feels that the reading of a section of the novel is superficial, imaginative involvement inadequate, or that pupils have not been aware of the implications of the scene. By exploring through improvisation a situation closer to their own experiences, students can establish connections between the novel and their own lives. One of the issues in *Frankenstein's Aunt* is the way rumours can fan feelings and lead people to form opinions not necessarily based on first-hand experience. The experience of other people talking and spreading rumours about them (or their friends) is one which pupils can relate to, and improvisation around this theme can clarify the villagers' feelings and reactions when they are sitting in the pub talking over the arrival of Hannah Frankenstein.

Apart from key moments, or themes, pupils often have a superficial understanding of a character. By piecing together a character's past from hints and references in the story, the pupils can begin to assess and understand them, and understand why they feel and behave the way they do. They can recreate scenes from a character's past, introduce new characters or use minor characters to explore unwritten scenes perhaps alluded to in the story. Through role-play and interaction, they come closer to understanding the characters, motivation, social contexts and relationships. Take for example the character Mr Evans (in *Carrie's War*). The pupils could consider his past life and recreate scenes from it; they could examine his public and private faces; they could set up situations that have him interacting with major and minor characters in the novel – and thus move beyond early stereotyped impressions of 'Mr Meanie' to a fuller and more sensitive understanding of this character, who by the end of the novel is seen in a more complex and sympathetic way.

'Hot-seating' of characters at key moments (possibly with two pupils representing a corporate character for mutual support) can help throw light on character motivation and pupils' perceptions of a character. Such activities need not occupy a great deal of time, and may be best tackled just after reading the relevant episode: Gryce could be 'hot-seated' after the caning incident in *A Kestrel for a Knave*; the father in *Welcome Home, Jellybean* could be questioned about his decision to leave his family; does Michael really mean it when he swears to kill the soldier in *A Game of Soldiers*? These can be done informally, as part of a lesson, or set within a wider drama context – an inquest into the death of the soldier (*A Game of Soldiers*) or journalists trying to probe behind the facts of the explosion at Annerton Pit (in Dickinson's book of the same name). When the context is wider, then a range of minor characters can be included for questioning.

Use of a 'distancing' role, where the class considers the characters or events from a perspective outside the novel, frees pupils from the narrative line and allows speculation. For example, a court of inquiry into events can summon characters – social workers, doctors, counsellors, psychologists – to give evidence and help get to the bottom of an incident. During a reading of *Of Mice and Men*, the pupils could be cast in role as doctors and social workers trying to decide what could or should be done with Lennie. The teacher-in-role as one of the committee could challenge their ideas and offer solutions they found unacceptable; the class would have to rely on their impressions of Lennie using the novel as the basis for their information, yet they would also have to bring what they know and feel as people to their arguments with the teacher-in-role. In cases like this, although the drama is rooted firmly in the text, the pupils are moving outward towards universal concepts – a process which can be achieved through discussion but which is more accessible through drama as feelings become refined and articulated concretely.

Minor characters, as well as contributing to inquests or talking to reporters, can also meet together to discuss their view of a major character or event. For example what might Joe and some of his crowd, or Beef and his cronies, say when discussing Neil and Geraldine, or the incident in the cafeteria in *Welcome Home, Jellybean*?

In some novels the actual dialogue is difficult to interpret and blocks the pupils' access to the experience of the novel. Here it will be necessary to demonstrate that there are meanings behind the words; the pupils can realise the variety and range of interpretations that can be drawn out of dialogue (and description) – from the literal through to the symbolic. As Frank Kermode points out in *How We Read Novels*, when reading there is 'always a requirement that the reader be a more or less sophisticated interpreter' and drama can help the pupils to create and explore their own interpretations of dialogue and to become aware of the variety of interpretation, rather than to be told this, or have it teased out in once-removed discussion. By experiencing the power and possibility of dialogue and word interpretation, the pupil becomes her own meaning-maker.

Two books I have found that present problems for class use because of the dialogue are *The Owl Service* and *Red Shift* by Alan Garner. In order to demonstrate the power of dialogue and then relate it to the text I have found the following method a useful approach:

1 Exercises (removed from the actual novel itself) in which pupils explore responses to snippets of dialogue, in order to create the awareness that reading requires a degree of interpretation. Pupils can be asked to make up short dialogues, or examples can be given out:

e.g. **A**:   Going then
    B: Maybe
    A: I thought I'd wear this
    B: Very nice

When pupils read these dialogue snippets at first, they assume an attitude or mood and convey that. Then you can ask them to build in the way they feel about each other, then location, then relationship (family? peers?) – each time keeping as much from the previous layers as possible. As the pupils begin to make the dialogue their own, they realise that four lines convey many layers and levels.

The teacher can move on from this point by asking the pairs to invent their own dialogues and present them in a series of different ways, each with its own meaning. The context and relationship must be clear in each different situation. An alternative could be to provide a short dialogue for a small group to build an improvisation around. If the dialogue is sufficiently ambiguous, the class can share and discuss the inevitable range of interpretation.

2 The same exercises can be applied to the actual text itself – taking lines from a novel and exploring how to say them in order to convey layers of meaning and relationships. Pupils will have to interpret, empathise and use knowledge of the characters to convey these layers of meaning. Although these are exercises, and the affective experience is not fully realised, nonetheless such work is valid: if lines from a novel are treated in isolation, when seen in the context of the particular scene of the novel the pupils can begin to realise that to understand not only the words, but what lies behind the words, needs more than a superficial reading.

The two examples which follow illustrate some 'activities whilst reading a text'. The first example uses a distancing role and explores pupils' perceptions, as themselves and as others, of characters in *A Kestrel for a Knave* by holding a case conference on Billy Casper. It also has built-in possibilities for written tasks which could form part of G.C.S.E. coursework.

The second example is a much more detailed and analytical account of the planning, implementation and evaluation of some sessions on *Lord of the Flies*. This example is more of a documented case study, and grew out of an INSET programme – hence there were two teachers (myself and the class teacher).

A Kestrel for a Knave – Barry Hines

The class was quite difficult to motivate, uninterested in written work, and contained some strong anti-school characters who were always ready to disrupt the work. They required careful handling and treatment, and I was well aware that 'drama' (as they perceived it) would be viewed with suspicion, hostility or at best apathy. I decided to use role-play which would be tightly structured and non–threatening. We were about two-thirds of the way through *A Kestrel for a Knave*, and they were quite amenable to being read to, but less willing to talk – and quite resistant to writing!

Bearing this in mind, I decided a 'Case Conference' would be quite a good vehicle for allowing everyone to contribute to a sharing of views on the characters, and especially for exploring a range of perspectives (including their own) on Billy. However I decided not to create their roles by outlining a situation as teacher–in–role; instead I opted for role cards, and a highly structured organisation, so they would be able to see what we were about from the start. The framework was as follows:

1 Outline idea of a 'case conference' on Billy – purposes. Explain some will be the 'committee', others will be characters from the novel who are invited to talk to the committee about how they see Billy.

2 Allocate roles – ask for volunteers. If necessary allow two people to represent one character. Give out role cards. Read them out (or with pupils) and ensure everyone understands what they are supposed to do.

3 Allow preparation time. Support and advise where necessary – both individuals and the committee.

4 Committee interviews characters in turn (they decide order). Keep notes on each character's perspective and evidence. Others can watch this.

5 Committee have chance to recall any character for further questioning.

6 Committee to discuss and make a recommendation.

7 Open discussion on the process, and how it helps our understanding of the characters and of Billy. Were the characters role-played in keeping with how we see them in the book?

8 Written assignment, possibly for inclusion in G.C.S.E. folders: 'A Social Worker's Report on Billy, which explores his family, school and personal life.' *OR* 'A collection of documents that were used in the Case Conference: School Report, summary of family circumstances, etc'

Although the context was artificial, it succeeded in getting the class to talk and discuss. The situation aroused and held their interest, the level of thinking about characterisation and themes was far deeper than any previous discussions, and everyone contributed something. With another class a tight structure and role-cards would not have been necessary – but with classes not used to role play and perhaps self-conscious about what 'drama' might ask of them, a tight structure can prove effective.

Below are some examples of the role-cards I issued.

> You are X. You have been invited to attend the Case Conference that the Social Services Committee are convening on Billy Casper. They want to find out as much as they possibly can about him with a view to deciding what could be done to help him, if he actually needs any help or support.
>
> Please think carefully about what you might want to say about Billy, and be prepared to back up anything you say or to explain your views.
>
> For example . . . (information/questions relevant to role).

The first type of card was allocated to Mr Gryce, Mr Farthing, Mr Sugden, a local police representative, the Careers Officer; a social worker, Mr Porter (the shopkeeper). Each card had some more individual pointers for the specific role. Billy's mother and Jud had slightly more informally worded cards.

> You are Billy's mother. The Social Services Committee are holding a Case Conference to discuss your son. You may not really know what this means and may be a little unsure of what they are doing and why they are doing it. They could ask some very personal questions and you will need to think carefully about what you are willing to tell them and what you either prefer not to tell or think is none of their business. What do you feel about the situation? About Billy? About having to attend this conference?
>
> Use what you know of Billy's mother from the book in order to respond as you think she would.

The members of the committee had a more detailed role-card.

In practice each character was role-played by two members of the class, and time was allowed for each pair to practise their role and the interview together. In the final phase of the work, I joined in, in role,

---

You are a member of the Social Services Committee who investigate and consider cases about children and young people referred to you by social workers, teachers, probation officers, educational psychologists and even parents. Your job is to consider the needs and well-being of the child (or young person) and make recommendations that will be of most benefit for that person.

You have been given the case of Billy Casper – a 14-year-old boy. You will hear from his family, his teachers, other people who have had contact with him, and from Billy himself. On the basis of what you hear you will be asked to recommend short and long term proposals for Billy's welfare.

Decide the order in which you wish to hear from people, and how you will organise the Case Conference. It may be helpful to draw up a list of questions – general ones or ones for particular people.

Should you wish to interview a character again (in order to check some facts or confront them with new evidence you have been given since their first interview) you may do so before making recommendations.

---

as a member of the committee who was quite reactionary ('lads like this need locking up . . .') which certainly provoked thought and discussion on a wide range of options!

Lord of the Flies – **William Golding**

Members of the department were very keen to try out ideas floated in discussion, and I was able to arrange to work on this project alongside a colleague in her classroom. There is tremendous value in this kind of collaboration: we jointly planned and taught each session, and our planning for subsequent sessions meant we had to evaluate together what had been happening. Each session is described in four phases – the aims and issues needing attention; the strategies to facilitate exploration of these; the working plan; and a description and evaluation of the session as it actually turned out.

The class was a fifth-year, all boys, 'low-ability' set. They had a reputation in the school for social, behavioural and motivation problems. They had difficulties in both reading and writing, and found it difficult to remember events and sequence in a story. They had just started reading *Lord of the Flies* (and were already finding it difficult), and the class teacher was hoping to eventually set a written task on the characters of Ralph, Jack and Piggy which some of them might submit for a C.S.E. English Folder. The sessions took place in a small, cramped classroom, with old-fashioned furniture, and lasted for 70 minutes each.

The drama activities are part of other activities, and the lesson plans and evaluative descriptions show these transitions between role-play, reading of the text, writing and discussion.

The planning

The information the class teacher supplied set the pattern for the work – it had to concentrate on Ralph, Jack and Piggy. We were tied to the pace at which they were reading the novel, and the first session was due to take place just after the boys had finished reading chapter four. This would mean that key areas, such as the Beast symbolism, could only be touched on. Although the sense of the unknown and fear is important, the characters of Ralph and Jack in a sense represent the conflict between 'civilised' feelings, rules and order, and freedom, emotion and anarchy. Was it possible to encourage them to be aware of this? The class teacher's comments also gave another thrust to the work – to consolidate events and actions, and their reactions to these, from previous reading.

It seemed crucial to get the group to work out for themselves why the characters reacted and felt as they did, and this could be highlighted by examining Ralph's and Jack's feelings and motivations at key points – e.g. the end of chapter one, and the final confrontation before Jack leaves the group. Could the boys bring together and consolidate what they had picked up from their reading so far, and predict what might happen? By letting them decide what they thought should happen, to predict both as themselves and as characters in the book, there would be a reference point when they came to read the next chapter.

Session One

Aims
● To check what the boys remember and think is important in the first four chapters.

● To consolidate what they already think about Ralph, Jack and Piggy.

● To anticipate what might come next.

● To understand Ralph's reactions and Jack's reactions to the fact the fire is out.

● To think about what the other boys in the novel feel about the obvious tension, and about Jack and Ralph, at the moment when Ralph calls an assembly (at the end of chapter four).

● To make the experience of the boys' feelings in the mountain come alive and be personal to the group. To imagine not only what they felt, but also why.

Strategies
- Chairs arranged in large circle – furniture pushed well away.
- Still Image – firstly the group to sculpt two teachers as an example, and secondly in their own groups. (Detailed on pages 39–42.)
- Soliloquy – to imaginatively recreate feelings.
- Pair Work – in role as minor characters.
- Concrete Symbol – conch shell.
- Teacher-in-role as Ralph – to inject tension, provide concrete focus.
- Written Task – to allow a developed and considered individual response.

The Plan
1   Pupils in circle, furniture removed. Discussion to establish significant events, and what the boys remember from chapters one to four: names, situations, how they got there. Teacher one to ask group to 'remind' him – place the onus on them.
2   Explanation of 'still image' idea as a useful focal point to establish what people are thinking/doing. Moment under consideration is when Ralph sees ship and realises there is no smoke. If necessary refer to text for what he was doing at this moment, but see if boys can supply this first. Class teacher, and teacher one to be Ralph and Piggy; class to mould and discuss how they should look.
3   Soliloquy – ask teachers to speak aloud their thoughts. Get suggestions from boys first. Discussion of why they feel like this.
4   Recap events on mountain top, in sequence, from when Ralph arrives until he calls the assembly (last half of chapter four). Try to get boys to remember the events and sequence (Jack and Ralph argue; Jack smashes Piggy's glasses; Jack apologizes; the fire is lit; the boys eat meat; Simon gives meat to Piggy; Jack says 'do our dance'; Ralph calls an assembly). Groups to choose a moment from *anywhere* in this sequence and re-create in a still image. List main events on sugar paper first?
5   Share images. Soliloquise as many as possible (if they can cope). Hot-seat one or two characters? Establish what is going on in both Ralph's and Jack's mind.
6   Discussion on the above – focus on why and how Ralph and Jack differ.
7   Build up pig-killing chants. Establish rhythm and pace, let chant build up. (Not necessary to 'act' this!)
8   Chant interrupted by teacher one in role as Ralph, holding conch aloft. Use actual words from text – calling an assembly.

9   Pair work. Not as main characters (Ralph, Jack, Piggy), but as other boys walking down the mountain, discussing events on mountain top, feelings about it, about Ralph and Jack, and Ralph's interruption and calling of an assembly.

10   Discussion to share above work. Written task (in role from pair exercise) – thinking over events as you walk down the mountain to that assembly.

Evaluation of Session One
Despite my initial apprehension, the group are extremely co-operative and we establish an informal rapport smoothly and quickly. The boys remember quite a lot, and just need triggering. They seem to enjoy being the 'experts' on the book telling me about it, and although several gaps need filling, we move effortlessly into the first stage of the work.

Being in 'control' of two teachers is a task they enjoy immensely – the sculpting of the still image is punctuated by laughter, but in a purposeful not a destructive manner. They are able to ease into the situation in a way that does not expose them, and the comments as to what is in Piggy's and Ralph's minds are rooted in a clear grasp of the significance of the situation and an understanding of the characters.

'What the hell is going on?' (for Piggy) is, in their own language, an accurate assessment of Piggy at that time. As the sculpting progresses they move deeper into the two characters bringing in what they know and infer; they are simultaneously inside the situation, and outside it. There is a concern that it should look right:

'Piggy looks too comfortable', and they supply the ideas for the teachers to use in soliloquy.

This work gives them a secure base from which to work out their own still images, which are carried out with control and thought. One group asks the class teacher for her glasses (and is very careful with them) and during the planning of the work and setting up of the images all the boys are totally involved. One boy is initially unhappy – 'I don't wanna do it' – but within minutes this boy takes the lead and organises his group! This group in fact volunteered to show their image. In the first image shown through the boys are asked to identify who is who – and why:

'That's Simon – he's sitting in amazement.'
and in the second image the group are asked to touch a character whose thoughts they want to hear. This group had chosen the smashing of the glasses moment:

Ralph: What's goin' on? [*Looking amazed at Simon*]
Piggy: He's just a bully. [*Recoiling from Jack*]
Simon: It's all your fault. [*Pointing at Jack*]

Jack: You've had it now. [*Moving aggressively towards Piggy*]

They draw heavily on their own experiences, but nonetheless link this to an awareness of the tensions in that moment.

The boys move into making the chant 'kill the pig, cut her throat, spill her blood, bash her in' – and circle round the room saying it. They are obviously self-conscious here, but the class teacher capitalises on this with:

'Who feels daft? Who didn't really want to join in?' and links this with how some of the boys may have felt. Connections are made between themselves, the 'drama' and the experiences of the boys in the book all the time, as they move in and out of the book.

The chant is built up again, and there is a genuine response of shock, surprise and confusion when I interrupt in role as Ralph, holding aloft the conch and calling an assembly (the actual words Ralph speaks in the book were used here).

In discussion the boys considered why Ralph did this:

Pupil One: Everyone's doing what Jack wants to do – not what Ralph wants.

Pupil Two: He's feeling ignored.

Pupil Three: Jealous.

Pupil Four: They should have been at the fire.

Pupil Five: He's had enough of what they've been doing.

Teacher: Any other reasons?

Pupil Six: Call order to them all and sort them out.

Teacher: What was the important thing they'd forgotten? [*Pause*] What was the significance of the fire?

Pupil Seven: They couldn't be rescued.

They have clearly grasped the implications, they have made inferences about the characters, and have started to be aware of the reasons why Ralph and Jack come into conflict – based upon their own opinions, rooted in their own experiences but also within the book.

The boys are asked to write their thoughts in role as they walked down the mountainside (the pair exercise has, unfortunately, to be cut – the class is summoned by the Deputy Head to the hall for a 'serious matter'!). The pieces, despite mechanical and technical problems, show the boys moving close to a personal understanding and viewpoint of that situation, as the following extracts illustrate:

'. . . just because he can't have fun like us he had to spoil it for everyone, I hate him . . . I don't want to go to a boring assembly . . . don't it make you sick, its silly having to hand the conch around all the while . . . I hope Ralph tell's Jack off for letting the fire go out and for hitting Piggy and all that . . . I felt amazed, but with Ralph as the leader he must have something important to say . . .'

I reproduce in entirety the following piece (from a boy in a 'low-ability' English set remember). I think the piece needs no explanation; it has the power to speak for itself. This boy has been given the vehicle for an individual, personally felt response and seizes it:

> Spoilt sport Ralph
> Him and his damn conch
> Why should we go?
> Why should I go?
> Up on the mountain we were free
> Free from life and it's rules
> But now we have to land back down
> to civilisation, where the rules are,
> Where disciplin is.
> We were free,
> I want to be free!
> Anyway who cares
> Not I
> Not anybody.

Session Two

All of the aims established in the first session had been achieved. In addition the group were enthusiastic, co-operative and totally involved. The book had started to live for them. It was now important to develop the responses, opinions and ideas emerging on the characters, and the situation.

Aims
● A reading of their written responses provided the main objective for the session. The boys demonstrated a feeling of sympathy for Jack. It was now important to get inside Ralph and try to understand him. Was he just a 'spoilsport' who felt left out?

● To anticipate what they thought might happen and compare it with the actual text. (Focus on the assembly Ralph calls.)

● To pinpoint the differences between Ralph's and Jack's attitudes, and articulate their own feelings about this.

● To make the reading of the text enjoyable and also significant.

● To consider how the others might feel about Ralph and Jack and what is happening.

Strategies
- Visual symbol of the 'conch' – to be used in discussion and to create a 'feel' for the assembly?

- Hot-Seating of Ralph (teacher-in-role).
- Teachers-in-role as Ralph and Jack.
- Boys in role –
  (a) as important named characters
  (b) as 'littluns' or unnamed characters
- The text itself – dramatised dialogue reading.
- Creation of unwritten scenes.
- Discussion out of role.

The Plan
1   Discussion of last week's work. Try to consolidate ideas about the feelings and motivation of Ralph and Jack.
2   Teacher one in role as Ralph – holding conch. Thinks aloud about the assembly (using Golding's words). Boys able to question him by 'hot-seating' process. Moment is just before the assembly convenes – emphasis on Ralph's inner conflict – need to put things straight – but can't think like Piggy.
3   Group in role as boys at the assembly. Teacher-in-role as Ralph goes over his points (using actual words from the text). Second teacher in role as Jack mutters (as does Jack in the text). Allow discussion on fear – 'this is what we can talk about'. Conch to be placed in circle and see what happens!
4   Dramatic reading of dialogue from this assembly on the fear by the teachers. Discussion outside the drama on why, what, significance. Relate back to them in role during stage 3.
5   In threes, Jack, Maurice and Roger discuss the assembly and their view of what happens and should happen, and their feelings.
6   Sharing session of previous group role-play – probably by discussion, but if the boys do not feel self-conscious or threatened perhaps some could 'show' us? (Danger of this 'showing' is that it is difficult to recreate the moment and the spontaneity.)
7   Group to be 'littluns' – using conch, holding own assembly and discussing the events, the situation, the fear and their feelings about Ralph, Jack and Piggy.

(Another option, after stage five or six could be to ask the threes now to become Ralph, Piggy and Simon, and explore these boys' feelings as they talk in role about the assembly. This shift of frame would sharpen the perspective and possible differences in attitude. However, time will dictate whether this is feasible to do.)

Evaluation of Session Two
The lesson starts with a recap on last week. The boys show a fusion between their own experiences and understanding from the drama coupled with an accurate and detailed recall of sequence and incident:

Pupil One: Jack said he was sorry but didn't mean it.

Pupil Two: He assumed that as soon as he said he was sorry it'd be okay.

Teacher: Good. Yes.

Pupil Three: Ralph called the assembly and interrupted.

Teacher: We started to think about that?

Pupil Four: They were all excited . . . he wanted to calm them down.

Teacher: Why? . . . What are Ralph's and Jack's priorities.

Pupil Five: Being saved.

Pupil Six: Having fun . . . going hunting.

I then become Ralph in a 'hot-seating' process, and the class teacher prompts the questioning. In role as Ralph, I use Golding's words to answer and indicate Ralph's thoughts. The pupils question Ralph and listen carefully to the replies; sometimes defending themselves:

'What are we doing now?'
'We were having a good time up there – you've spoiled it all for us.'
'We was only having a little dance.'
'You've had all day to call the assembly – why do you call it now?'
'We won't let the fire go out again though, it was just an accident it went out.'

Interestingly the pupils unconsciously ask questions as themselves yet also in role as the boys! A discussion follows on what the group have found out about Ralph.

Teacher: What sort of things seem to be going on in Ralph's mind?

Pupil One: Confused.

Pupil Two: He's prepared and they ain't.

Pupil Three: He's the leader, and they're not doing what he says.

Pupil Four: They're thinking about fun all the time.

The class teacher narrates as preparation for the assembly, reminding the group of their own feelings (emerging from their writing), and asking them to wonder about what Ralph is going to say. She builds this by a series of rhetorical questions designed to help them prepare and remember their reactions. As Ralph, holding the conch and using actual words from the book, I go over the main points Ralph makes – fire, shelters, water, toilets. The class teacher in role as Jack pretends to be bored, interjects 'too many things', mutters, whittles a stick.

Still as Ralph I say 'we can talk about the fear'. Jack (the class teacher) picks up the conch and uses Golding's dialogue where Jack turns on the littluns and comes across as a blustering bully. Conch left – no one takes it up! We wait, sense the boys are uncomfortable and feel exposed so break for discussion.

In this discussion the group freely and openly consider what they have just seen and heard, and what it shows them about the characters.

Teacher: Who was it mainly concerned with the beast?

Pupil One: Jack.

Teacher: Who was he trying to convince?

Pupil One: The littluns.

Teacher: And where had they got the idea?

Pupil Two: Well they says that they seen it.

Teacher: Have they seen anything do you think?

Pupil Three: No.

Pupil Four: Some creature? . . . Or dreams? . . .

Teacher: Can you imagine Jack comforting the littluns? What did he say to them?

Pupil One: Told them they made it up and to forget it. Shouted at them there was no beast and if there was he'd found it.

Pupil Two: He's not afraid and doesn't like anybody else to be afraid.

Pupil Three: Everyone should think the same as he does.

Teacher: What do Ralph and Jack seem to be like? How do they come across?

Pupil Five: Almost arguing.

Pupil Six: Their ideas are different.

Pupil Seven: Ralph sees the problems.

Pupil Five: And Jack sees the fun of it.

Teacher: How does Jack feel about Ralph?

Pupil Two: Don't like him.

Pupil Eight: He's jealous of him.

Pupil Five: He thinks he's wrong and Jack's right – he was chief of the choir – he's done it before, he should be in charge like.

Teacher: How did he seem to be reacting during Ralph's speech?

Pupil Two: Bored.

Pupil Five: Not interested.

Pupil Nine: Not prepared to listen to what anybody else has got to say.

Pupil Two: He's made up his mind that whatever Ralph says is not going to make any difference, he believes that Ralph is wrong.

The discussion probes their understanding, and the responses clearly show a deep awareness of what the undercurrents and tensions are, and why they are there – as the extract clearly shows – they had listened to and watched the dramatised reading intently, both picking up facts and interpreting them.

As teachers we continue to read aloud the dialogue. Interestingly, when Ralph asks for a vote on ghosts several of the group raise their hands (a response this time to the invitation to join in!). Jack makes his dramatic announcement 'Bollocks to the rules' and whoops off. The final part of the chapter where Ralph, Piggy and Simon discuss what to do is read aloud.

This final stage could have been anticipated and explored by asking the boys to be these three characters discussing Jack and the assembly in role. However, we decided at the time that the next stage was important and that to be Ralph, Piggy and Simon, then Jack and two friends, was too much of a shift. In addition time was ticking away! The reading had been significant – and the ensuing discussion on that final stage demonstrated clearly how much the boys had absorbed. Ralph is 'disappointed' and 'wants to give up', and doesn't blow the conch because 'they're all gone – that's it'; 'he's scared no one will come back'. Piggy is 'scared Jack will get him', and when asked why Piggy is afraid and wants Ralph as leader – 'Jack and Ralph are strong people – he's not because of asthma'; 'he has no standing. Ralph and Jack they're leaders, but Piggy is nothing.'

The class teacher then asks the boys to consider what 'the other side' would be saying, thinking and feeling. The boys get into groups of three or four as Jack, Maurice, Roger (plus another choir member – Bill?) and discuss in role their attitudes to the assembly, to Ralph and things in general. We go from group to group, in role as one of the choir, supporting, structuring, challenging as necessary.

Realising that showing will serve no purpose – spontaneity will be lost – we ask each group to report back their discussion. I hand the first group the conch shell . . . (and produce a full transcript here because in many ways it speaks for itself and demonstrates the depth of the work):

Group 1

Spokesman: Why should we have rules? If there are two separate groups Ralph can go on his own, he doesn't have to follow us.

Teacher: So you're saying then there should be two separate groups . . .

[*Pupil One passes conch, shuffling about till Spokesman Two finally holds it.*]

Group 2

Spokesman: We talked about who should be leader, Jack or Ralph. There are too many rules, why should we have rules! Why should we have a fire?

[Passes conch, *laughter – who will hold it? Spokesman Three takes it.*]

Group 3

Spokesman: I should be leader – Jack should be leader – and there's no need to build the huts because we can sleep near the fire to keep dry and toilets – that's ridiculous going all the way down to the rocks just to go to the toilet – doesn't make sense at all. We didn't help build the huts but there again he didn't help us hunt, yet he's eaten our pig and that. I should be leader – I can have more better rules than Ralph – he's got silly rules.

[*Passes conch which is naturally and easily accepted.*]

Group 4

Spokesman: We talked about the beast and if it was true and who believed it and who should be leader. We weren't certain who should be leader . . .

Teacher: Did you decide what the beast was?

Spokesman: We decided it weren't real.

[*Passes conch (this convention now totally accepted).*]

Group 5

Spokesman: We believe we shouldn't believe in this [*indicates conch*] at all. Some of the rules are quite stupid. We should make Jack the leader – he makes work a pleasure.

It is interesting how one boy (3) reports back half in and half out of role at first, and by the end of his report is firmly in role. The conch is accepted, and the ideas expressed are quite obviously their own feelings and responses as fifth-year boys to the book, the characters and the situation. These ideas are expressed clearly and fluently, confidently and carefully. The discussion continues, reflecting back on what they have just explored in role in order to sharpen their responses and clarify them. What happens in the rest of the book will be no surprise – inevitable really – they sense it themselves already, in role and out of role! In this discussion the boys seize the initiative and the conch becomes an important control device, as the transcript shows:

Teacher: Anybody talk about Piggy? [*One hand raised – before he can start he is given the conch by a boy on the opposite side of the circle, who says* 'hang on a minute' *as he walks over, giving it to Pupil One.*]

Pupil One: We talked about it if I was leader I'd put Piggy down, probably even beat him up – I don't like Piggy!

Teacher: Why does Jack hate Piggy so much?

Pupil Two: [*Takes conch from Pupil One.*] Because he's got brains about him. Whereas Jack wants to have fun killing pigs and stuff.

Teacher: Is Piggy a threat to Jack?

Pupil Two: Not really.

[*Pupil Three walks over, takes conch, returns to seat.*]

Pupil Three: Piggy won't actually be a threat to him it'd be more like Piggy would know what to do and Jack knows that Piggy knows what's right but it's not what Jack wants.

Teacher: So you reckon Jack thinks Piggy is right?

Pupil Three: Yeah.

[*Pupil Four signals for conch to be passed to him.*]

Pupil Four: I think Jack doesn't like him because when you look at him he's the odd one out. He's not like the rest – he's built differently – he suffers from asthma – he's always moaning. He says all the *right* things . . . Jack thinks maybe he can't think as well as Piggy – he always thinks about going hunting.

Teacher: Piggy says all the right things? What do you mean?

[*Pupil Five moves forward and takes conch.*]

Pupil Five: He sounds like a grown up and he acts like one – he kind of speaks sensible like.

Teacher: Oh – so he says all the 'right' things, and this is a reason why Jack dislikes him?

[*Pupil Three walks over and takes conch again.*]

Pupil Three: Jack seems to think that to be leader there's no need to have any sense. All you need to be leader is to be bigger than everyone else – if you're stronger than everyone else that automatically means you are a leader.

This discussion shows a highly articulate understanding of the characters. Pupil Three's final comment is universal and places the experience of the book firmly in the boys' own perceptions of human behaviour and their own experience. The discussion is a direct result of the way the reading and thinking about the novel have been structured: the barriers of language have been crossed; the boys are firmly *inside* the book and relating to it, drawing from it, internalising the experience and understanding it. This high-level discussion and concise perception demonstrates clearly how an unmotivated 'switched-off' group *can* be articulate, empathise and be given the means to express themselves.

The class teacher closes the lesson by asking the group to imagine the littluns have got the conch and are having their own 'meeting'. Unfortunately the bell finishes the lesson after only three comments, but these comments illustrate the boys' ability to see and understand another viewpoint:

Pupil One: I don't think Ralph's been a good leader 'cos no matter how much he says he's the leader Jack's still going round bullying people. He thinks he's dead big and all the biguns has been bullying us littluns and we don't seem to have any say in what's going on around us. I don't think they're being fair to us.

Pupil Two: I'm scared. Not only of the beast but of Jack. Jack's a bully and if he gets to be leader he'll bully all us littluns. He never listens to what we say at all – at least Ralph listens to us.

Pupil Three: I think we should give Ralph a second chance in what he's doing. Listen to him and obey what he says instead of going off all the time.

Clearly the boys are able to support Jack, yet see through him. They are aware of the tensions, the range of attitudes, the divisions, the emotions, the anger, the uncertainty. Unconsciously, in the final discussion as themselves, the conch takes on a significance – they in fact hold their own assembly! The lengthy transcripts are included here to demonstrate the extent to which the aims of the session have been realised. They require very little analysis – the boys' own words, in and out of role, clearly show how involved they are in the work, the book, the experience; they are 'active meaning-makers'.

Session Three

The group have proved very co-operative and manageable – they are very willing to try activities provided they do not feel they are 'acting' to an audience. They have a definite feel for the use of the conch, and understand the idea of working in and out of role as a means of looking back, exploring a section and anticipating and analysing both the book and their own experiences.

Aims
● To explore the key section, where Jack *openly* challenges Ralph's leadership, through the questions: Why does Jack challenge Ralph? How does Ralph feel? How do the other boys react? Why? Why was the challenge not immediately accepted? Why did most later join Jack? What are the implications of this?

● To explore the above questions by allowing the group to recreate that challenge, make their own decisions – what would *they* do and why? To examine the text and see what Golding makes happen and consider any differences.

● To see if any boys can cope with being 'key' characters, without reliance on teacher-in-role.

● To consider what effect the challenge will have on succeeding events – not only 'why?', but 'what now?' How have past events been leading to this point?

● To develop the personal responses of the class, and enable the boys to make their own meanings, both inside and outside the experience of the book.

Strategies
● Boys in role as major and minor characters.
● Still-image – to focus on a key moment – freeze the action.
● Hot-seating and soliloquy.
● Writing in role.
● Chapter 8 used for reference.
● Conch as a symbol – concrete and abstract.
● Reflection out of role to clarify thoughts, feelings and understanding of recreated events.

The Plan
  1   Offer roles of Ralph, Jack and Piggy to volunteers. (If no response at all, teachers will function in role – but judging on the past contact it seems likely that there will be no problem here.) Jack to be

briefed by one teacher, while the other teacher narrates for rest of group the events on the mountain top when Ralph, Jack and Roger find the beast (parachutist). The boys have not quite reached this point in their reading.

2   Jack blows conch and calls assembly. Makes the following points:
(a)   We've seen the beast – it raised its head at me, Ralph and Roger on the mountain last night.
(b)   Ralph is a coward – he hung back.
(c)   Ralph has insulted the hunters . . . leading to:
(d)   Challenge – who thinks Ralph shouldn't be chief? Jack to hold conch during all this.

3   Freeze at the moment challenge issued. Hot-seat Ralph, Jack and Piggy – feelings, motivation, attitudes.

4   Jack to repeat challenge – Hands up if you think Ralph oughtn't to be chief. Allow vote. Freeze – soliloquy and hot-seat boys at assembly. Teacher to ask for thoughts, and probe with questions – why have you voted/not voted?

5   Hot-seat Ralph, Jack and Piggy again after boys have voted. Others can answer for them by walking up to character, placing hand on shoulder and assuming that role. What are you thinking? What will you do now?

6   Discussion out of role on events created, attitudes manifested, and significance of the challenge and what they decide happens. Read Golding's version in chapter eight. Compare with their decision. What will happen now? What will be the effect of Jack walking off? What will Ralph do? What will the others do?

7   Inform them of the fact that boys do drift off and join Jack (even though they didn't vote) – why? Refer back to their own drama. Why did/didn't you vote? Where is your sympathy? What does this signify -- a turning point?

8   Writing *in role* as one of the boys after this assembly – thinking over the events and what you will do now.

Evaluation of Session Three
This final lesson proceeded very much along the lines of the original structure, but with the addition of a pair exercise (one supporting Ralph, the other Jack) just after the assembly breaks up.

Three boys quickly volunteer to take on the roles of Ralph, Jack and Piggy. While Jack is briefed (which could have been done with a role-card) the class teacher recaps events, narrates and sets the scene. What are *we* thinking about? Jack has called this assembly is it usual? Is the beast real? (Rhetorical questions – boys internalise responses.)

Jack enters, holding conch.

Jack: I'm calling this assembly, not Ralph. I've actually seen the beast on top of the mountain – Ralph's a coward – he hung back – he was the first to run away. And he's insulted your hunters, he thinks they're no good – but they're good hunters. Who thinks Ralph shouldn't be chief anymore? I should be chief. (Teacher stops it. Asks Jack to repeat his last points. Anybody like to ask what is going on in Jack's mind?)

Teacher: What would you like to ask him?

Pupil One: Why do you want to break us up when Ralph's doing all right? You're just trying to get revenge as far as I can see.

Jack: 'Cos Jack's *not* doing all right – he's calling the hunters no good – they're good hunters. Ralph isn't a leader – I should be leader.

Teacher: Why do you think you're a better leader?

Jack: I'm stronger. I'm in charge of the hunters. I'm better!

Teacher: What's going on in your mind Ralph?

Ralph: Why's everything gone wrong?

Teacher: Piggy?

Piggy: Now we'll never be able to get back home.

Teacher: Jack will you ask for the vote again and we'll see what happens.

Jack: Who wants me to be chief? (Two boys raise hands.)

The class teacher then tells boys she will ask them to speak aloud their thoughts – among the responses are:

For
Because I'd be one of his hunters, he'd be doing well.
He's stronger and I like him more.
Against
I want to be rescued – he doesn't care.
Ralph's doing a good job.
He's doing all right.
Ralph is a sensible leader.

Teacher: Is that what you expected, Jack – only two people?

Jack: No I expected a lot more.

Teacher: How do you feel now?

Jack: Disappointed and let down.

Pupil Two: He looks a bit of a fool standing there. Opened his big mouth and nobody voted for him.

Teacher: Piggy – how do you feel now?

Piggy: Relieved!

Teacher: Ralph?

Ralph: Great! I hope they think I can do a better job. I want to carry on, keep the fire going, get things back into order, things are getting out of hand.

Teacher: What will you do about Jack?

Jack: He might come slamming across to me and take the conch, 'cos he knows now all the others support him.

Teacher: What about the rest of you? What do you think Jack feels or will do.

Pupil Three: Keep quiet for a while.

Pupil Four: He's going to feel left out.

Pupil Five: Feel offended.

Teacher: Jack – would you like to do and say what you feel you would?

Jack: Well, if that's what you think you can keep your damn conch and your chief.

[*Throws down conch and storms out.*]

Clearly much is happening here. The boys speak confidently in role, showing an empathy for and understanding of the characters, again drawing on the book and their own experiences. Their answers show perception and sensitive awareness of the situation, from Ralph's anguished plea 'Why's everything gone wrong?', to Jack's 'keep your damn conch'. Interestingly the vote had gone very much as the Golding version – which is now read and discussed.

In the discussion about the events the boys draw heavily on their observations and responses to their own work –

> They didn't vote for Jack 'cos if he was leader they'd have a bad life – he doesn't want to be rescued.
> Ralph's not actually done anything wrong. It's a risk with a new chief.
> He called it at the wrong time – he just came out and said it all – he planned it wrong.

One boy asks what time this took place, checks with the book, realises it is dawn and says 'So they were just waking up? Maybe they were still asleep.' In ten years of working with this book, this simple, yet very significant fact had never occurred to me – he clearly uses the textual information to make a deduction – a very valid one. The few pages forming this incident gradually take on more and more significance for the group, as they tease out interpretations and make hypotheses.

I ask Jack to repeat his words when he walked out, and replay it for us, and we will see what happens.

There is a long pause. I gently pressure Ralph 'What you gonna do, Ralph?' – in role. Ralph picks up the conch, defends himself against Jack's accusation and asks others to comment. Piggy picks up the conch and speaks in support of Ralph. I press again, in role, about the beast. Ralph asks the hunters to support him and help him kill the beast.

The class teacher then explains that in the text, boys drift away and join Jack. She asks the boys to get into pairs and discusss what to do, one is sympathetic to Ralph, the other to Jack. We go from pair to pair, in role, supporting whichever is the weaker partner, challenging, probing, wondering – depending on the way each dialogue is shaping.

In the open discussion that follows, the boys reflect on the work with their own ideas and opinions feeding and being fed by their knowledge of the characters and the incidents. Comments include:

> 'We were on the spot like'
> 'I didn't want to offend Ralph – I want to be with both!'

They reshape the experience and make it their own, but there is a problem in trying to recapture all the good points spontaneously talked about in the pair role-play exercise. An extremely interesting comment emerges near the end of the discussion, when one boy reminds everyone that it is a nuclear war in the world outside – so what point is there anyway in going back? What will there be worth going back to? The boys might as well stay and have fun. From his viewpoint, rooted in his own impressions of the world in the 1980s, Ralph's values and attitudes have no place in a world that has destroyed itself.

The class are then asked to finish the session, by writing their thoughts in role, after witnessing Jack's challenge.

I saw Jack standing with the conch, shouting that he should be leader and asked us to vote for him, but nodby did note for him. I did not vote for Jack because I was half asleep and it came so suddley. Whe I thought about it Jack was right that he should be the leader because Ralph spoils all our fun, for all we know we might not even be rescured and we will get bored with Ralph.

I had been woke up very early in the morning to go to an assembly, at first I thought he was Ralph who was holding it, but I was rong, Jack was holding it. When we get there Jack started babling about being the chief, he asked for a vote to get rid of Ralph, but know bode put there hand up.

Jack looked abit disapointed and shouted at us pour boys in discust then he said, 'I'm going off by myself if aneybody wants to joyn me they can. I wanted to joyn him but how, I didn't vote for him so how.

After the meeting I swanked off to try and find Jack and I did in the woods.

Jack called a meeting in the morning it was too early to have a meeting so I wasn't thinking abot what he was saying. After Jack went off I realized what he said was true and I wished that I had gone off with Jack and not stayed with Ralph not wanting to offend Ralph I slip out into the forest to my surprise I was not the only person that had joined Jack.

I didn't want to hurt Ralphs feelings. Jack alway's gives us fun but I can't fight him because he's a bully and he's too strong. If I ever got to dislike Jack Ralph would soon take me back Wheras Jack would not let you if it was the opposite way around. I want to be ralph's Friend but I also wanted to hunt With Jack and dress up and paint my face. With Ralph its boring because you have to away I keep the fire going, and you can never hunt or have a war.

I was surprised that JACK called the essembly and evenmore shocked when he wanted us to vote for him to be chief. But I needed time to think about my vote and I was afraid to vote at that time. I also feel unisided because if I go with JACK ill have a good time. AND if I go with Ralph I have a better chance of being rescude. (SORRY ABOUT BAD ENGLISH)

I was sitting there starring at the grass, but I was listening to Jack.

I didn't vote for Jack because all he was worried about was that Ralph called us names, but when someone is mad they say a lot of things that they do not mean.

I enjoy to hunt but oned say I want to get of this island and Jack isn't worried about his parents or his family who are back home. Another thing is that he is a bully and I would not like him bulling me all–day long telling me to do this and that!

I didn't vote for Jack at the time as I didn't really have the chance to do so as it came all of a sudden it just came out, And I didn't really no what to say but now I have had a good think I have decided that.

I have reproduced these pieces as originally presented, in order to contrast the boys' confident talk with their struggle to control the written word. Despite the technical problems, each pupil has communicated their own interpretations of the experience, and made their own meanings. They are themselves, yet also the boys on the island; throughout this project they are both inside and outside the experience of the novel.

After-thoughts on the three sessions

At the very end of session three, the boys were asked to jot down their feelings about the lessons and whether or not the work had been useful, interesting, enjoyable, helpful. Their perspectives on the work are refreshing and illuminating:

'The teachers have been great to me in these drama sessions. I have understood more about the story. Because just sitting down reading a book isn't very interesting but sitting down talking about it and drama-ring it has been very enjoyable.'

'I have learnt more about the characters and how they felt. It makes you want to be there to make the difference.'

'Found the different things difficult at first – get used to thinking not what you normally think but to think how the characters think.'

'These lessons have gave me great pleasure as well as letting me understand the book and help me do my essay work better.'

'I was not here for 3–4 weeks and having these lessons has helped me a lot. Because when we read the book I can't understand anything.'

The class teacher had not intended reading all of the novel – but the boys demanded it, and the writing produced during the sessions shows a struggle to communicate their personal and felt responses. They bring to the talk and the writing everything they know as themselves, and tie this to the experience of the novel; though writing presents problems for many of the group the pieces have power and honesty. Significantly, when freed from the pressure of always writing, or writing in a 'pseudo-literary' style, the talk they engage in both in and out of role allows them to both understand the experience of the novel and make it their own. The drama presses them to find words to articulate and shape these meanings – through public and private talk, conversational and semi-formal talk they respond both as themselves yet also in role – in one moment able to sympathise and identify with Jack, yet in another moment able to be highly sensitive to the emotional turmoil of the littluns. Strikingly they also LISTEN – synthesising what they hear with their own feelings and ideas as they internalise the whole give and take of conversation.

· The project was also a learning experience for both me and the class teacher – we had to think carefully about how to facilitate responses to the text without imposing our own perspectives; we had to study the text together, as well as with pupils; we had to learn about collaboration and working together in a classroom; we jointly evaluated what we had seen and heard. What started as an informal arrangement has now become an integral part of a departmental approach – sharing, talking, planning, teaching and evaluating *together*.

7

Reflections

Activities after reading a text

Strategies and approaches

If a novel is to have impact and be absorbed consciously, there needs to be time to reflect after reading so that the teacher can challenge, and deepen the pupils' initial responses. There must be a process of sitting back from the experience of reading, and time to consider. Reflective activities using the drama process allow the reader to hold the novel in her mind as a whole work, and to use everything she has picked up about the characters, themes and incidents in a way that will involve her at a personal level, rather than in abstract once-removed discussion.

Drama allows the pupils to be both inside and outside the experience of the novel, and the interplay between the book, individual response, and shared response will lead to a deeper understanding of the novel as a whole. Through role-play, the pressure will be on the pupils to pose questions, make decisions and take responsibility for the initiative – and the teacher will receive valuable insight not only into pupils' interpretations and understanding, but also into what the story has actually meant for them; often there may be a discrepancy between what the teacher thinks the pupils have enjoyed, understood or found worthwhile, and what the pupils actually think!

One process which moves readers on from the situation of the book is for pupils to invent their own drama from the implications the story holds for their own lives. After reading *The Silver Sword*, the themes of friendship and loyalty could be explored; or the issues of leaving home and family tensions could be the focus for work after reading *The Green Leaves of Nottingham*. The teacher's responsibility will be to focus and direct the learning so that the drama experiences become meaningful, rather than staying superficial and stereotyped.

The story itself can be viewed from different angles – perhaps using pupils' understanding of the characters to create unwritten scenes that might be hinted at or alluded to in the story, expanding minor characters, introducing new ones, or even changing the outcome of the story!

Alternatively minor or secondary characters, real or invented, can discuss a major character. How would Buddy's school acquaintances discuss him at various stages of Hinton's novel *Buddy*? What would

94

be the responses of the twins to things other characters might say, feel or ask about Buddy? How do characters react to his disappearance?

Straightforward activities such as freezing a scene and questioning the characters are useful ways of viewing characters at different stages in the book: alternatively, pupils can construct a series of still images of moments they consider key moments in the novel. These still images can be given functions which subtly alter how they are chosen and presented: perhaps illustrations to accompany a deluxe edition of *The Lion, The Witch, and The Wardrobe*; still photographs to advertise a film version of *A Pair of Jesus Boots*; museum exhibits (e.g. tapestries) on *The Children's Crusade*; a photographic exhibition on life in the Wild West using *Shane*. Where characters and key moments from the actual text are represented, then the scene can be brought to life. If it were possible for the characters to alter what happens, what changes would they make and why? Titles for the still images can be chosen and discussed – such strategies lead back to interpretation and the text itself, and simultaneously give the teacher access to what the pupils think, feel and understand from their reading.

For example, what would the father's response be in *Welcome Home, Jellybean* to questions about his decision to leave the family? What still images would convey his most vivid memories? If Tran, in the novel *Escape*, were looking back over the events of his flight from Laos, his stay in the Malaysian refugee camp and his early days in America, what still images would encapsulate his experiences? What would be the inner thoughts and feelings of each person in those images?

Small group or pair work can be set up so that, for example, a reporter interviews a central character to obtain the inside story with human interest. This can be developed to include interviews with bystanders, minor characters, or additional invented characters, who have a necessarily limited view of the events. The aim here is to encourage speculation about and interpretation of a variety of attitudes to events. This reporter role can be given more credibility if the reason for the interviews is built into the role and is appropriate to the fictional situation: a contemporary teenage magazine writing about young detectives for *Mike and Me*; a gatherer of local stories and superstitions for *Frankenstein's Aunt*; Chroniclers for *Viking's Dawn*; keepers of the archives for *A Wizard of Earthsea*. After reading *Eleanor, Elizabeth* by Libby Gleeson, a local journalist and photographer could come and interview Eleanor, Ken, Mike and Billy about their miraculous survival of the bush fire. These interviews could extend to parents, school friends and minor characters in order to get at the 'inside story'. By making the role appropriate, belief can be built; there is a concrete reason (within the drama) for the interview to take place and be recorded.

In order that the whole class can share such activities, the pair or group interview work can take place in a larger context. For example, the teacher-in-role can function as magazine editor or head keeper of the archives and collate the sharing of reports. (It may be more effective to be the secretary or the scribe and allow a pupil to handle this role. There is the danger that teacher-in-role always adopts a role very close to her own role as organiser and dominator of the activities. The role of amanuensis hands over initiative and responsibility to the group.)

These approaches can form a base for more detailed and extensive activities. A useful structure that can provide a central focus is the making of a drama-documentary programme that uses characters and incidents in the novel alongside researched 'factual' information. (A version of this approach was referred to in the planning of work on *Carrie's War* where one possible framework was to mount a museum exhibition – see p. 51.) The novel is the 'human' resource, and interviews, photographs (still-images) and 'home-movie' clips can be woven into a more ambitious structure. *A Question of Courage*, for example, could lend itself to a drama-documentary about the life of Emily Palmer, and the characters and incidents from the novel would be meshed in with other contemporary material on the period and the Suffragette Movement.

A G.C.S.E. class who had read *1984* worked on producing a short T.V. programme for The Ministry of Truth. In this case, the class was split into two groups, but though neither group knew it, each had a slightly different task. The first group worked on the 'official' Government vidi-cast; the second was asked to prepare an 'underground' programme. The pupils drew on characters, incidents, symbolism, power structures and language from the novel, and in each case had to demonstrate and use their knowledge of the book and their abilities as language manipulators in a highly specialised way. The teacher role I adopted was that of an officer in Internal Security who was sympathetic to the 'underground' group but aware of the consequences of any support, and who thus voiced vague hints to the 'loyal' group. The two groups had to co-operate and share their ideas – but of course the unofficial vidi-cast had to be kept secret while the loyal party members began to be suspicious about the actions of the other group. Here the drama was rooted in the context of the book, yet we also began to create our own drama about suspicion, loyalty, trust, idealism, conviction . . .

Throughout this kind of activity, the pupils are encouraged to refer directly to the book, elaborate detail, make inferences about characters and their attitudes, and actively involve themselves at an emotional level; at the same time using retention of story-line, plot, incident and characterisation to inform and shape their work. Importantly, the very nature of such tasks imposes specialised language demands and consideration of style, structure and communication of meaning become consciously significant.

Another easy and effective situation to organise is a 'celebration party' where characters meet to talk over events. It is helpful to use this as a starting point and then to shift the perspective to the future. A distant perspective in time allows reflections on the actions and events as a whole. What would Mary and Peter say and feel about their experiences twenty years after the events in *Walkabout*? How would Bill tell his son about life before and during the breakdown of the world in *Day of the Triffids*, if his fourteen year old son asked him? What would Bill say – and what might he leave unsaid? If mediums or supernatural phenomena experts began to delve into the events as described in Westall's *The Scarecrows* some two years later, what would characters say to them? What would characters ask them to try to explain? How might they begin to piece together and explain the events? Such activities will require the pupils to make connections between what they already understand and any detailed knowledge of the text they have acquired.

An extremely effective way of bringing about interplay between the novel, individual response, shared response and pupils' own experiences is to set up a trial, tribunal, case conference or enquiry with the whole class. There is no need to emphasise detailed procedure; the enquiry mode itself is what is important.

One of the examples at the end of this chapter documents and evaluates such a method. After reading *The White Mountains* the class, in role as Council Members, questioned Will, Henry and Beanpole just after their arrival at the Refuge. Chapter Nine describes how such an enquiry was incorporated into work on *A Wizard of Earthsea*.

With *Lord of the Flies* I have used the enquiry mode, splitting the class into three groups:

(i)   Some of the survivors – Ralph, Jack, Roger, Maurice, Sam 'n' Eric, Littluns (e.g. Percival).
(ii) Parents of the boys (including Simon's parents and Piggy's aunt).
(iii) Government officials, social workers, psychologists, medical staff.

The situation was that the boys were about to arrive at a reception centre, staffed by group (iii). This group were given a list of boys on the plane, a list of survivors and the naval officer's report. Their job was to interview and examine the boys, find out as much as they could, and decide what, if anything, should be done. Parents had been informed and were ushered into a waiting room at the centre, told the boys were expected shortly but nothing else. The boys were told to give an account of their 'adventure' to the committee before being re-united with waiting parents. I was secretary to the reception centre team, enabling me to liaise, pass messages, support and place the onus on the pupils to create the work and make their own decisions.

Intense and often heated discussion and questioning took place: the parents demanded to see their loved ones and objected to being kept in the dark; there were discrepancies in the boys' individual accounts; the committee was divided over what to do. The 'action' was fast and furious, with all pupils staying firmly in role, using the incidents of the story and bringing in their personal view of these. They had to make meaning from the experience of reading, and drama gave them the vehicle to be both inside and outside the experience of the book.

The next two sections document ways reflective activities such as these can be structured: the first uses drama as a means of encouraging pupils to consider not only the characters and situation of *Welcome Home, Jellybean* but also to confront the issues of handicap, disability, and how they respond to, feel about, and handle these; the second example produces a detailed analysis of the planning and actual practice in two sessions on *The White Mountains*.

Welcome Home, Jellybean by Marlene Fanta Shyer

We had just finished reading the novel. The class were totally silent, immersed in personal thought about the novel. Usually they were quite rowdy, and eager to disrupt anything they saw as 'boring', but the reading of this novel had subdued them considerably. Because of the emotional impact of the narrative, previous discussions had been stilted, and one boy, whose sister was in real life handicapped, had found the experience almost traumatic. The class had been unaware of this until his angry, savage verbal attack on another boy who commented on 'spazzies'.

Before reading the novel, we had created a drama which explored attitudes to a proposal to establish a Half-Way House for handicapped and disabled people in a residential street. Although it had revealed prejudices, the class hadn't really engaged with the situation. It had not gone especially well, and many of the responses were shallow and stereotyped.

Since beginning the novel, the atmosphere had changed: no one laughed at or mocked Geraldine; they all seemed touched by the experiences in the novel. However, their responses were being internalised. Could they talk about the events and characters in a non-threatening way? Had they made any connections between the real world and the fictional world of the book? How did they *feel* about the family's decision to bring Gerri home? How much had they understood of each family member's complex and ambiguous feelings for each other and Geraldine?

I punctuated the silence which followed the finishing of the novel by posing the question – 'I wonder what happens now', and after a pause . . . 'is this a happy ending?' As usual the confident and articulate offered views, the vast majority were still silent. I needed to create opportunities for all to speak, but in a way which would offer some security . . . and the notion of trainee counsellors, willing to listen and offer support to a family as part of their final training phase, was the framework I chose to open up reflection on the novel and the universal issues. The trainee frame allowed us the freedom to not have correct answers or the pressure of being expert, and the distancing of this frame from the novel would, initially, allow us to discuss general issues before tackling the key moments of the novel.

Framework

1   Teacher in role convenes session for trainee social workers and counsellors. Part of final training phase – begin to deal with real people and their problems. Introduce first practical idea – pensioner who lives alone, recently burned himself whilst cooking. Two people to visit him at home, talk to him, see what support they can offer and what help he needs.

2   Ask for two volunteers. Still in role as training officer, explain you will be the pensioner. The class, sitting round in circle, can stop role-play at any time, or the two volunteers can stop the drama to ask for help.

3   Interact as recalcitrant, stubborn pensioner with the two trainees. Possible actions: don't answer door; be unwilling to open door; you don't need any help, people should mind their own business.

Allow drama to develop, but be prepared to stop and come out of role and discuss what is happening, or try some parts again.

4   Discussion, in role as trainees, about this kind of problem and how to handle it, and how it was handled. Anyone else want to try?

5   Pair exercise. Quickly give A and B the following information, separately. (Role cards are useful for this kind of exercise.)

A. B is going into hospital at short notice and no one has made arrangements to look after their one-year-old daughter, Tara. The husband/wife is working abroad, and there are no relatives nearby. You have to explain to B that the toddler will be temporarily taken into care until B is well enough (approx. one month).

B. You have suddenly been informed you will have to go into hospital for about three weeks, due to a nasty fall. Your wife/husband is unable to return from her/his work overseas for at least a fortnight. You have a one-year-old daughter, Tara.

What is important is the discussion after the role-play exercise. In role as trainees, pupils reflect upon the kinds of feelings displayed by the B's; the way A's handled the situation; how each person felt about the other; the range of possible responses to the information; and any compromises or alternatives reached. Pupils consider the kinds of skills the trainees need for situations like this, and any conflict in their own feelings.

Then, still in role, link into the next phase.

6   *The Oxley family* – The Oxley family have taken their daughter, Geraldine, who is mentally handicapped, out of state care and are looking after her at home. Since that time the family has now split up (Dad no longer lives with the family), and the son's schoolwork appears to be suffering. We are going to find out as much as we can to see what help or support, if any, can be given to this family. The first job will be to find out how they feel and how they've been coping.

Now will be the time to break the drama, and organise out of role. Ask for three people to each represent Neil, Mum and Dad. Who else might be able to give information? (Such people as Mr Rasmussen, Mr Parrish, Mrs Shrub and Mr Guttag can be lifted straight from the novel. Other characters could be invented – a close friend of the mother, another neighbour, Gerri's teacher, etc.)

Assign each character a small group to interview them. Each character will need time to prepare what they may want to say – and refer back to the text – and the counsellors will need time to prepare questions and decide what they need to know and how to find it out

7   Allow counsellors time to talk to characters.

8   In role convene large meeting (of whole class as trainees). Share the factual information and impressions of characters, etc. After this, move on to considering the family situation. Are they coping? Is this the best place for Gerri? Is it fair on Neil? Can Mum continue alone? Why did Dad leave? Would Gerri be better off in residential care?

Teacher role here can put pressure on the group – e.g. pushing the idea that the family can't cope (cite Neil's school problems, Dad leaving, neighbours' complaints) and that Gerri shouldn't stay in the family (unsuitable accommodation; she'd be better off with the right facilities and trained personnel).

The White Mountains by John Christopher

The group was a third-year mixed-ability class – minus the most able children – who had just finished reading the novel. The framework was designed to encourage reflection on the story and to stimulate interest in the two sequels. The structure describes two 60 minute sessions, which took place in an ordinary classroom. The first session was extremely difficult – some pupils were disruptive and silly – and the second session was planned to tackle the problem by deepening commitment to the drama and building belief in it.

The planning

The aim was to enable the class to explore their attitudes to the story and the characters, and to hold the book as a whole in their minds. What had they understood about the characters of the three boys, their motivations, and their attitudes to each other and the world they inhabited? What would be the problems faced by these characters now the journey was over? How much had the pupils assimilated of the narrative sequence? How could they be encouraged to demonstrate this knowledge and understanding?

Very little information is given about life in the White Mountains; there are just a few scant paragraphs at the end of the story that look forward to the future. This seemed to be the starting point. What sort of community was it? The book tells us nothing about life there, the problems, or the future (this in fact is done in the sequels). How would this community respond to the new arrivals? Would they trust them? By building a picture of life in that community and then 'examining' the three new arrivals, I hoped to make the pupils fall back on everything they remembered from the reading, to empathise with the situation and characters and to move them to consider some more universal ideas – friendship, betrayal, loyalty, and trust. The situation would also stretch their language usage – they would not only have to find appropriate language but actively use it in a range of functions – questioning, probing, reporting, recounting, persuading, convincing, justifying, explaining.

Session One

Aims
- To build roles as preparation for the next session.
- To use clues from the reading to consider the kind of community this might be, its organisation and problems (especially survival), the life of people inside and outside the community.
- To test pupils' understanding of the context of the story and cappings, tripods, etc.

Strategies
- Class all to have roles as members of the community, but will

work in groups who choose specific responsibilities (i.e. opportunity for them to negotiate their roles).

● Teacher–in–role as Council Leader, to co-ordinate, link and build belief in pupil roles.

● A meeting where groups share ideas and report.

● Writing in role to clarify thinking from the session, and help create details for an authentic community.

The Plan

1   General introduction to role-play and the rules of the game; establish the contract. Establish teacher-in-role and 'stop drama' signals; (exercise where I interact in role to give idea of this).

2   Informal discussion with the class to tease out the following points:

(i)   What do we actually *know* about this community (use text); what can we surmise?

(ii)   What is life like there, what problems do the people face? (Combination of text and hypothesis.)

(iii)   What kinds of special skills will be needed? What sort of allocation of responsibilities for organising life would there be?

This to be collated on the board to provide a visual focus.

3   Class to form groups and choose a specific responsibility e.g. shelter, defence.

4   Teacher-in-role as leader of the Council to set scene and organise tasks. Communicate in a worried manner that there is rivalry and discontent among factions, and some antagonism towards the Council. There is to be a full meeting where everything will be open – every group will inform the community what they are actually doing, what grievances (if any) they have, what problems they are facing in this responsibility, what items of equipment, etc. they need.

5   Groups prepare their reports (in role) for the Council meeting, and appoint a spokesperson. Teacher stays in role to support and sympathise with a group's problems and to help provide structure if a group needs it. (Although the meeting itself could have provided tensions, I had already decided to inject a common focus by interrupting the meeting with an urgent problem.)

6   The meeting of Council to be convened, and the discussion to start.

7   During report back I will be summoned urgently away, quickly returning to inform community that we have an urgent problem (*defence?*) – a foraging party is 12 hours overdue and there is suddenly a lot of Tripod activity on the valley floor.

8   Class in role allowed time to question me to clarify situation and problem.

9   Short open council meeting, then I will ask groups to go and work out proposals for what should be done – as quickly as possible! Perhaps establish priorities and immediate problems – defence, evacuation, emergency plans, etc.

10   Meeting where proposals shared, and a strategy drawn up for Council to implement.

11   Reflection on the session. Discussion to focus on the hardship and problems of the life in the community and why people chose it. Written task – diary entry of a fairly typical day in your life as a member of the community.

Evaluation of Session One
The lesson proceeded very much along the lines of the plan: the class were quite happy to be organised inside a structure. In many ways, however, the session was extremely difficult. Some pupils found it easier to disrupt the session than commit themselves to it. These problems were exacerbated by the fact that the session was the Friday afternoon before half-term. However, much interesting and valuable information emerged, and a session I thought rather a failure, was seen differently by the pupils.

It was clear during the opening discussion that the pupils had never thought at all about the community that Will, Henry and Beanpole had struggled so hard to reach. They began to remember clues from the closing pages of the novel, and built up a picture of a community isolated, threatened, concerned with safety and survival. The groups chose to be responsible for defense; food rations; health and education; scouting parties; researching ways of dealing with tripods; supplies. Groups got going and were able to function without interference from the disruptive boys (who banded into one group). The following comments are culled from notes I made during these group discussions:

> 'Place more lookouts around the mountain, get more trained men, disguises, camouflage.'
> 'Warmer clothes are needed.'
> 'We must make or get more false caps.'
> 'People in the villages are not putting their washing out – they know we are taking it. We need warmer clothes and the little kids should be warmer especially babies. We need woolly clothes and blankets.'
> 'Clothes are getting torn and there is no way of mending them.'

The boys who had banded together did not really try to be serious at all in this group work. Although they were able to be serious when I spent time with them supporting them, they generally were unable to believe in their task – even though defence was something they chose for themselves.

The Council Meeting was ragged and noisy, but my announcement succeeded in providing the focus and attention needed. The next phase of group work proceeded more purposefully and seriously. Even the difficult boys were able to work – although they were still occasionally disruptive. The group discussions had the focus necessary for the class to work in a way that engaged them. There was less tendency to gossip or chatter and the talk was geared, for most groups, entirely to the problem. The groups noted down comments such as:

> 'Where is they (the Tripods) week points. We now they can walk threw water but can they walk threw fire or slipery oil?'
> 'Send a good actor down as a vagrant to find out what is happening.'
> 'Everyone must be ready to fight, but what weapons can we use?'
> 'This is how the new lookout rota will work – two people per lookout post, starting from sunrise to noon, noon to sunset, sunset to midnight, and midnight to sunrise. We must make a good alarm system to warn everyone if there's trouble.'
> 'Send our best trained men down . . . meanwhile move the women and children to higher ground.'
> 'Camouflage the entrance with more snow, hide all tracks.'
> 'We must plan an emergency evacuation, but where can we go?'

The comments and group discussion made in the initial part of the session showed an awareness of the problems facing the community; the comments in the second half show a shift – they used knowledge of the book (Tripod abilities, vagrants, etc.) and combined this with knowledge built up during the first half of the session.

The final meeting was more orderly, but by now the class was impatient to start the half-term holiday, so the reflection was superficial. The written work they produced however was a pleasant surprise – it consolidated the work of the session, sharpened perceptions about the kind of community being portrayed, made pupils think back over the story and use this information to make guesses about lifestyles and problems based upon their own ideas, the book and the drama experience. One boy (who had been *really* disruptive) wrote 'it had been boring for me this week because I had all privileges taked off me for sounding the alarm for no reason . . .' – obviously using his own experiences and relating them to life in the community! Interestingly he later refers to the Tripods having burnt something in the valley 'I think it was a cottage we don't know why this happened it just does every month or so (wierd ain't it?) . . .' – an idea not mentioned in the drama but which is referred to very briefly in the book. He had remembered it, and used this in his writing.

The following examples (reproduced in their original form) show pupils using this process of drawing upon the novel, the drama experience and their own experiences to shape and give form to their response.

1   It was early in the morning, two people were just leaving for the village. While they were gone, we were choping logs down with flint from the mounting. our idea was to place them at the top of the hill and when a tripod came we would let them roll down and knock them over. all of a sudden the ground shuck, there was two tripods in the valley as if they were searching. we ran to were the logs were stnding and wited. They started to move again towards the village. anly one of the people returned from the village and told us that the other one had been captured and caped by a tripod.

2   It was my first day in the White Mountains and I was frightened and confused. It was like a bad dram that couldn't escape. I couldn't get to sleep at all, and I didn't want to. For I was afraid of the drams I might dream. Which seemed so real. The dreams that would wake me up sweating from fear, crying out, reaching out for the ones I onced loved who are now gone. In the morning it was cold and dull. Icicles hung from the cave entrance. Even your breathe froze in the air. It was if Spring would never come. I used to watch the elders going out early in the morning and not coming back until night. It was if they would never come back at all. Sometimes they came back with a stag hanging from 2 wooden sticks. It's side was bleeding alburnuntly from the wound, it made me feel sick, but then sometimes they came back with nothing. So we had to do with fruit and roots or cook veg. For the first few days I did nothing, but on the next day I was given a certain job to do. I was to help the women make the clothes. I weren't all that much cean on it, but I new I couldn't argue with the panal of elders.

3   I awoke by a ray of light which was peeping through the cracks of my little cave. A typical day ahead of me nothing tremendous or exciting was going to happen, it never did in the White Mountains.

All I did was obey Orders, my job was to keep the people of the White mountains healthy which meant going down to the valley everyday picking plants to make medicine with, and cutting down willow trees, to make asprins. The men helped to chop down the trees, which made my job easier. My biology lessons in the past were Very useful, I had to know which plants were safe and which weren't.

I would gather the plants and take them upto the White Mountains by feet.

105

I was a very busy person. With the plants I had gathered I would crush up and make medicine.

I would treat many people everyday to make sure they hadn't any disease, as it was very easy to catch anything up in the white mountains.

My life isn't easy up in the white mountains, but what else? I don't want my mind controlled by the tripods.

I'd rather have my own thoughts even if they were *all* horrible.

I had come away from the session with mixed feelings, and a somewhat negative impression. The written work however (despite all the technical problems) made me realise much had been internalised. On reflection, I felt I should have done more to promote the disruptive boys' standing – they had chosen defence – possibly they could have been given a more concrete task such as drawing a plan and indicating what defences were where. Perhaps also the class needed time to assimilate or grow into their new roles as members of this community – a pair exercise where one shows a new person round, or a group still image (or series of images) showing aspects of life in the community could have been alternative strategies that could have been fed in at an early stage, and which another time round I would include. The class were not used to this way of working – I should have done more to ease them into it and help build belief.

Session Two

The class *must* be committed to the drama, must agree to work at and for it, rather than against it. Last week it almost disintegrated and was very hard work to keep together. Rather than tackle this outside the drama (though it must be mentioned), is it possible to build belief and commitment so that the drama experience and situation provides its discipline from within? Focus must now be switched to the arrival of the three characters to provide a new dimension to the work. The framework must facilitate both these aims.

Aims
● To re-establish the contract and tackle disruptive behaviour *within* the drama. To build belief and commitment to the work and the community.

● To use the sense of role and community created last session as a means of focusing on the arrival of three boys into this community.

● To get the pupils to use what they have assimilated about the characters, the plot, and the context so as to empathise in an imaginative yet demanding way.

• To consider the notions of trustworthiness, value to a community and freedom.

• To press them to seek appropriate formal language during the opening, then to ensure that in the group work that follows opportunity is created to use language skilfully to question, probe, examine, explain, regulate, inform, while the character being questioned will need to convince, justify, recount, explain, inform, re-tell – drawing on the book and their own experiences to give shape to this articulation.

Strategies

• Place some decisions on the pupils as a means of making it important to them (notably the opening) – it is *their* drama!

• Ritual of some kind to implement this decision in order to get individual and group commitment.

• An enquiry mode – characters to be interviewed about their story.

• Teacher-in-role as Council Elder – to control the ritual, and to inform the class of their task i.e. interview characters.

• Class in role as Council Members.

• Corporate character – Two or three pupils will corporately assume roles of Will, Henry and Beanpole.

The Plan

There is to be a ritual opening when work starts. I had the idea of an oath of allegiance, and the planning was based upon this. However, I did not wish this plan to be implemented if the class came up with their own strategy. The pupils would be asked to think over how members of the community *prove* their loyalty, or demonstrate it at least, and I will take their decision and build it into some kind of ritual. I will *structure their* suggestions. However an oath-taking is a potentially good strategy – so in order to illustrate how such a strategy can be structured the plan will assume this has been chosen. It is important to stress however that the pupils will *not* be asked to play 'guess what's in teacher's mind' – the decision *will* be theirs, not a con! The plan is an illustration of possibilities, or of a fall-back strategy if the pupils are unco-operative or unable to cope with making a decision.

1   General recap on last session. Specific mention of behavioural problems (without pointing blame at individuals) and lack of commitment. Perhaps it was the way the work was structured? To be dealt with initially outside the drama since the problem is serious enough to warrant this. The emphasis is on can *we* make it work – not on 'do it properly, or else!'

2   Discussion. Chairs arranged in a circle to allow all to contribute, feel a part of the process. How would WE prove ourselves loyal to this community or demonstrate loyalty? Class not in role, yet to be addressed in shadowy role – WE are all members – teacher with, not above, them. Gather suggestions – write on board.

3   Democratic process to choose one suggestion, or a conglomeration of suggestions. Possibilities may include a test, an oath, an examination, a trial period, etc. I may have to suggest voting – but will try to ask class *how* to reach a decision: the onus of making this decision will be placed on them.

4   Class to split into groups to work out suggestions on how the decision is to be implemented, e.g. to word the oath of allegiance.

5   Teacher-in-role as Council leader to refer back to rivalry, discontent and stress need for unity. Remind them of the way they demonstrated their loyalty when they arrived, e.g. the swearing of the oath, and ask that they repeat it publicly to re-affirm this loyalty. Will they agree to do so? (Loaded question this – I must be willing to face the consequences of asking them if they are willing. It must be genuine – and it is perfectly possible at this point that the plan for the rest of the session will be abandoned if individuals do not agree to this. The drama will then have to move in new directions – how do we get people to agree and what do we do if some do not agree – which is in fact a highly fruitful learning area.)

6   Assuming they agree – then the plan is to structure in a ritualistic way this demonstration of loyalty. Each individual will have to do so. E.g. they may have to walk up to the Council Leader, publicly swear the oath, be shaken by the hand and thanked for their loyalty and commitment. This may take a long time but it will be important to get it right – if necessary I will step out of role and discuss any problems with the class.

7   I will then explain to the Council that three boys have been found by a foraging party near our hideout and this has made the party late returning. In view of recent events (link back to last session) the boys have been isolated and separated until they have been questioned, and the Council will have to decide whether or not to permit them to join. Stress information from book e.g. they say they have 'killed' a Tripod – we have never done this – they are only boys! Can we trust them? Believe them? How did they find us? etc.

8   I will step out of role and discuss with class the task. Organise and clarify it. Ask for three volunteers to be Will, Henry and Beanpole, appoint two more to help each one. Remainder of class to split into three groups and be allocated one character to examine, question, debrief.

9   Provide written, simple, guidelines for the characters and the questioners.

10   Each character and helpers, and each debriefing team to be allowed time to prepare in role. Teacher-in-role supports Council groups where necessary, but also to support and question characters – how do you feel about being separated and locked up? Is this what you expected? Try to establish initial empathy with the character in this new situation.

11   Each 'character' taken to meet its committee and questioned.

12   Committees report back to full Council with information, recommendations, worries. Teacher-in-role to challenge, support and seek clarification where necessary.

13   Action based upon previous stage – perhaps the three characters will demonstrate their loyalty, whatever the Council decide!

Evaluation of Session Two

Firstly the plan was too far-reaching: there was not enough time to cover the last stages, and the examinations were still in full swing when the bell went, catching everyone unawares (a sign of involvement!).

The idea of a 'promise' (pupil's word) emerged very early in the discussion on possible ways of demonstrating loyalty, and the class quickly reached a consensus that this was what everyone should do. I did suggest a 'test' but the class ignored this – a promise was obviously something they had experience of, and they all felt that if people couldn't keep the promise they should be evicted from the community!

I asked them to work in groups and word this promise – which was done seriously and carefully as some of the final suggestions show:

'I swear to keep the secret of the people in the White Mountain and promise to defend our rights or another people's.'

'I agree to obey orders given out, never to betray my fellows and swear never to let out any of the secrets of the White Mountains.'

'I honour my tribe till I die, to tell no secrets to no other things apart from my tribe and I should help my neighbours from danger.'

'I promise to be loyal to my community and to die before giving the secrets of the community away. And to risk my life in the service of my comrades.'

The groups were given very little guidance beforehand and no help during the formulation of this wording. They used language in an unfamiliar way; all knew it had to sound right for a special occasion; this promise became important to them. They searched for

a correct vocabulary and syntax, with a content that fits the context –
drawing heavily on their own experiences (actual and second order
from reading and television), but meshing this in with the specific
situation. Comradeship, obedience, loyalty, co-operation,
responsibility and individual commitment were clearly
demonstrated in the context of the promises, and the syntax and
vocabulary were carefully chosen. They sensed it was important for
the drama to get it right – and they rose to this admirably.

There was no dissent in the final choice – each group read its
suggestion twice – and the choice was immediate and unanimous:

'It says it properly.'
'It's better 'cos we have to say our names.'
'None of the others mention the Tripods.'
'It sounds sort of serious . ! . y'know like swearing on the
Bible.'

The final choice was:

'I hereby swear, by the laws of the White Mountain, that I, . . .,
do commit my life for the safety of my new homeland, The White
Mountains, and will fight till the Tripods are no more.'

There was a sense of solemnity and seriousness here. The oath
contained its reason for importance: the tone was elevated by the use
of 'new homeland' and the formal syntax of 'I hereby swear' and 'till
the Tripods are no more'. The pupils realised this themselves as their
comments clearly show.

The ritual of the oath-swearing ceremony was carried out with a
great sense of occasion. Any giggles were due to embarrassment and
tension in the situation, not because it wasn't being taken seriously –
it was almost too serious – the pressure was real, inside and outside
the drama being created. This was not the same class as the previous
week – the work was important, they were ready to move to the
next stage.

The group questioning sessions were intense, and both sides (i.e.
characters and council members) stayed firmly in role, using and
drawing on the text both to pose and answer questions.
Unfortunately time ran out before we could reconvene to share, and
although we did try this in the subsequent lesson the intensity had
been lost. However the long time spent on the ritual *had* succeeded in
gaining pupils' commitment and engaging them in the work on both
a thinking and feeling level.

A colleague who had observed the drama sessions offered the
following evaluative comments.

'I was worried by the first session. I didn't feel the kids had
really engaged with the task, though I was impressed, and

surprised by the quality of the ideas in their writing. I wasn't sure how you were going to grip them in the second session, but you certainly did. The involvement in getting the words right really got that commitment lacking in much of the first session – and that oath was . . . well I couldn't have come up with a better one! And when they all had to stand up and say it – you could feel the tension in the room couldn't you? By the end of that they were ready to do whatever you asked.

The second part was excellent – that corporate character was far better than just asking one child – it gave it the depth, steadied it, and the mutual support really helped get into that character. Charlie can be such a silly little boy, but he was really calm as Henry, this was the first time I have ever seen him sustain himself in a situation.

The group of council members I watched closely were totally immersed in the situation. They really probed the character to find out if he was genuine, and they were really struggling to frame the questions in such a way as they would test the character. They kept turning to each other and trying to decide not only what to ask, but *how* to ask it. The corporate characters did the same – there was a reality about the situation that didn't stop.'

There was much interest when I showed copies of the two sequels, and they were in constant demand for the next few weeks. A book that the class hadn't really been very interested or involved in suddenly provided a new focus and impetus in our lessons as we turned our minds to gathering more information about the Tripods and making plans for defeating them.

8

Sumitra's Story

Text, Drama and G.C.S.E.

Drama and G.C.S.E.

With compulsory coursework and oral assessment forming an integral part of G.C.S.E., creative responses (especially to literature) are given status. No longer is the emphasis in English literature certification placed upon analytical essays; the criteria stress the development and expression of a *personal* response to literature. The end-of-course exam can create a situation where what the pupils need to know to pass the exam becomes more important than deepening their personal responses and enjoyment; coursework however allows pupils to respond in a variety of styles and forms – sometimes analytical or discursive – especially for the more able pupil – but also, significantly, 'recreative', so that pupils are able to produce letters, diaries, newspaper accounts, genre transformations, personal writing, invented scenes, etc. These pieces of work allow them to express their own interpretations. Drama strategies, such as those covered in previous sections, are designed to encourage students to create their own interpretations.

The National Criteria for English clearly spells out that English should be 'a single unified course'. In practical terms this means integrating language and literature work, especially as English coursework requirements demand pupils to respond to both literary and non-literary material. As well as emphasising the fostering of responsive reading, the criteria also require teachers to provide opportunities for wider reading (by giving them flexibility in the choice of books to be studied and not prescribing texts) and to consider how to meet cultural diversity. The criteria also indicate that language skills are inter-related and need not be assessed in isolation, but that teachers should seek to provide learning opportunities through contexts which clearly offer two or more of the opportunities referred to. Instead of compartmentalising English into reading, writing, listening and talking, the task facing us is to create opportunities for learning where the inter-related skills can be identified and assessed.

Additionally all pupils now have to be assessed in oral work, and the criteria here stress the inter-relationship between listening and talking, and the need to provide a variety of contexts for purposeful talk.

These needs – the development of a personal response to literature, contexts for a variety of purposeful talk and the integration of language and literature work through the complementary modes of listening, talking, reading and writing – are at the heart of the drama-based explorations that have been described in previous chapters. Many of the practical examples give rise to varied written responsive tasks, where the writing can deepen and enrich the drama experience, which has already encouraged reflection and personal response. The sessions on *Lord of the Flies* and *A Kestrel for a Knave*, apart from providing opportunities to share experience and response orally, also lead naturally into written assignments that are designed to encourage the more considered articulation of response.

Through drama, pupils are beginning to engage with characters, values or themes in ways that connect with their own lives and experiences – and the articulation of this response is achieved through talk. This talk may be tentative and loosely structured, or it may be quite formal with consideration of the right words and tone for the appropriate situation. Talk is central to the exploration of meaning within a text or situation, whether directly in role or by reflection out of role. It is the drama that provides the context for the need and opportunity to speak.

When pupils are engaged in role-play or discussion in role the teacher has excellent opportunities for observing and assessing the oral performance of her pupils – both listening and talking skills, individually or in small group situations. Sometimes this assessment can be carried out informally: individuals or small numbers of pupils can be closely observed and teachers can make assessments by taking notes or using a category or check-list system, depending on the situation. More detailed information to help teachers in making their assessment can be obtained by tape-recording pairs, groups or even the whole class and replaying recordings when more time is available to make a more considered assessment. A video camera can also provide a useful way of recording a session – though often in practice the sound quality is mediocre and the camera intrudes upon the work. However, it is possible to make tape and video recordings part of the drama process – some work on *1984*, for example, actually produced a tangible end-product (the party political video) which was used as evidence to assess a pupil's oral performance. This particular project used drama to provide talk as a product (the party video) and simultaneously allowed assessment of process talk through the variety of situations the pupils engaged in. I was able to assess pupil performance across a range of criteria, and to focus upon individual or group work as appropriate.

In this chapter I want to consider these issues in practical terms by taking a novel as the starting point for work which can be directly assessed and meets the criteria and syllabus objectives for G.C.S.E.

113

Specifically the work was designed to enable pupils to respond to the
reading of *Sumitra's Story* in ways which provided tangible outcomes
in terms of oral assessment, literature-based English coursework
and/or literature coursework.

Sumitra's Story by Rukshana Smith

The novel deals with an Asian family who have to leave Uganda
(at the time of Idi Amin) and settle in England. It is the story of the
oldest daughter in the family, Sumitra, who finds herself caught
between two cultures and who, ultimately, has to leave her family,
her culture and her home in order to preserve her independence.

I had only recently read the novel and was impressed by the open,
honest style through which the author communicates Sumitra's
personality, her anxieties and her doubts in a way which, I felt,
would be accessible to all readers. It faced key issues of racism,
gender, role, and the clash of cultural values in a way that did not
preach or patronise, and though I was a little unhappy about the way
the novel ended, I felt there was a lot here for pupils to engage and,
perhaps, to identify with.

Because the main character is a female Asian, (and a very
believable, forceful one at that) it immediately seemed to begin to
redress a gender and cultural imbalance in texts I had previously used
with the class (*Brother in the Land*, *Lord of the Flies*, *An Inspector Calls*),
and I was also interested in the responses of both the Asian and non-
Asian pupils. Would the white children develop a better
understanding of a different culture with which they came into
contact with every day, yet didn't really seem to understand or want
to understand? How would they perceive Sumitra's situation? How
would the Asian pupils respond? Would they feel comfortable in
explaining their culture and customs to the rest of the class? Would
they find the situation believable? How do they perceive the two
cultures they inhabit and how do they reconcile them – if they do?

The more I reflected on the story, the more qualms I had. Would it
create tension? What might be the response of some of the parents?
These doubts, paradoxically, made me more resolved to try out the
novel. There were plenty of common experiences – parental conflict,
family pressures and tensions, boy-friends, going out, independence
– which would provide a meeting point not rooted specifically in
cultural background. *But*, the fact that the context was a different
culture, a different set of values, customs, beliefs etc. was really the
key! To what extent would pupils empathise with Sumitra? Would
they understand the pressures on her? What would they feel about
her decision? Did they think she had any alternatives?

Through drama, I wanted to find ways to encourage pupils to

engage with the text at both a thinking and feeling level. This engagement would be developed through a combination of group and pair work, reflection, and discussion and writing related to the drama and reading activities. By using the immediacy of drama, I hoped to provide contexts for thinking about Sumitra's culture and the pressures she felt, and to allow pupils to find ways of articulating their understanding.

The ending of the novel required special attention and time would be needed for reflection on the whole experience of the book. I wanted this to be done in a shared way, through a drama-based experience.

Essentially then the drama work would have three main thrusts:

● To foster personal response and encourage reflection on the novel, and its connections with pupils' own lives.

● To provide a variety of different contexts, formal and informal, in which oral assessment could be made and recorded.

● To allow for flexible and personal responses to the novel which would be written but evolve out of the drama and reading activities. These written assignments should be capable of fulfilling specific syllabus objectives for either language or literature coursework.

The drama approaches and strategies I have discussed in previous chapters are not meant as a universal panacea, neither are they meant to replace other ways of working with a text. What they can do is to complement and sometimes deepen other ways of working, so that drama is not necessarily being used all the time (before, during and after reading) but is being used where the teacher feels it is appropriate. As I have argued drama can offer insights and experiences not so easily accessible in discussion or writing, and these experiences in turn enrich the reading, writing and talk centred on the text.

Establishing connections

I decided that all I wanted to do before introducing the novel was to find some connection between the early part of the story and the pupils' own experiences. I wanted then to get into the novel as quickly as possible, and was conscious of the initial resistance some pupils had felt when I had suggested the book to them for individual reading – they hadn't found themselves involved in the novel's opening setting in Uganda, but had become totally involved by the time Sumitra's family reach England. I wanted something simple, direct and non-threatening to quiet, shy pupils, and which would enable the class to identify with some elements of Sumitra's situation, no matter what their cultural background. The focus I chose was the feelings of a family who have to uproot themselves and move away from relatives and friends. I felt this was most easily managed in pair/small group situations, some of which I would try to tape-record to see how useful this method would be in providing tangible assessment evidence.

The structure I used was, essentially, as follows.

1 Pair work – (role themselves). Close friends – one tells the other that his/her father has to move (invent location and reason – but it's a *long* way away). Talk over the situation – how do they feel? Do they want to go? What will they miss? etc.

Discussion and sharing of issues and feelings arising from this.

2 Small groups – families. Packing up. For some reason it is impossible to take everything (haulage charges? Size of van that can be afforded? Air freight charges? Smaller accommodation? Renting furnished accommodation?). Allow groups to operate as families packing up – starting point given – Mum/Dad says 'Well we can't take that lot – only pack what you really need and junk the rest'.

3 Still-image. Each family looks at home they are leaving. Soliloquy – each person speaks aloud what is in their mind now, as they prepare to leave their home.

4 Whole class discussion, seated in circle. Share thoughts, feelings, perceptions and anxieties. Move in to real experience for those who are willing to share experience of starting a new school, moving to a new area etc.

I linked this to the book by saying that we were going to read a novel which dealt with how one family, and especially one girl, come to terms with a total change in their way of life when they have to leave their home and start again in another country.

Focussing on a key incident and characters

Once reading of the book was well under way most lessons were devoted to reading and discussion, normally with the whole class. This meant that two-thirds of the class made little oral contribution, so what I needed was to find a structure to allow everyone to contribute and to help them get inside the experiences by trying to understand why the characters act as they do. I also wanted them to root their talk in the context of information they had absorbed from the book so far. Again pair work offered security for the pupils and a common reference point in later class discussion. We had just read Chapter 10 (which explains Sumitra's father's attitude and some of the differences between Sumitra's lifestyle and those of her English friends, and also has 'tucked away' a significant comment from Maria about freedom to choose a marriage partner not necessarily creating happiness). In this chapter cultural values surfaced on which some role-play could be based and we could explore issues that the drama raised. I would also gain insight into pupils' understanding, empathy and perceptions. I asked the pupils to choose three different scenes, stipulating there must be one from each of two lists. We would share and discuss these, and I would set a piece of writing which would be based both in the drama and the actual text; and again I would tape some of the pair role-plays.

The structure here was as follows.

---

1   In pairs choose three of the scenes below. (One must be from A and one from B.) Decide who will take which role and spend a few minutes thinking about how the character will handle the situation, *based on what you know of them from the book.*

A
(1) Hilary asking Sumitra to go to the school disco.
(2) Hilary and Lynne discussing why Sumitra can't/won't come.
(3) Sumitra asking Bap [her father] if she can go to the disco.

B
(1) Sumitra talking over with Sandya [her sister] the school disco, and Bap's attitude to them and to English people.
(2) Bap and Martin discussing Bap's daughters, especially Sumitra, and Bap's view of life in England.
(3) Martin and Maria discussing their friends the Patel family and especially the way Sumitra appears unhappy.

---

2   Share with the class some of the improvised scenes and discuss how realistic the conversations were: whether they were 'in character'; how appropriate the vocabulary and content were; and whether they fitted into the pictures we had from our reading.

3   Coursework Assignment. 'In dialogue form, script three conversations that might have taken place between some of the characters during Chapter 10 of *Sumitra's Story* by R. Smith. Try to show clearly each character's attitudes, values and beliefs. Head each dialogue with a sub-title which gives the context.'

The dialogues that were produced were lively, and reflected much careful thought, drawing heavily on the pair work experiences. This assignment formed part of the syllabus's requirement for work based on the full reading of a text and since they had to draw heavily on what they had absorbed from their reading this could be used in either a language or a literature folder.

Moving out of the text . . .

Much later in the story, while Sumitra is working for Mr Farley's detective agency, she comes across a missing person file and some press cuttings about Asian girls who had committed suicide. This seemed crucial to Sumitra's own turmoil – she had not yet decided what to do – yet also to be more universal than the experience of the novel. I decided to use this starting point as the basis for an English assignment which would consist of several small assignments, growing out of the drama we would invent.

Initially I cast the pupils in role as trainee 'agony' columnists, who receive a letter from Varsha Nahri which is desperate, almost suicidal. My role was loosely defined as a problem-page columnist invited to lead this training session. In role we speculated on why Varsha felt like this, what pressures she might be under, and what answer (if any) we could give her. The letter was sufficiently open-ended to allow pupils to consider a number of pressures. They were then asked to write a suitable reply, which sub-groups (still in role) had to discuss with each other to consider its merits.

In the next session, I switched the frame and cast the pupils in role as social or community workers. I ushered them into a room containing a 'dead body' (the still figure of an Asian sixth-form girl). We left the room and I showed them the possessions of the dead girl – some family photos, jewellery, some personal letters and a stark suicide note saying 'I'm sorry – there's no other way out for me. I love you. Reema.' We speculated on reasons for her death and whom we would want to interview to find out as much as we could about the girl. I told them the father was in an adjoining room and he hadn't yet been informed of her death. Who would volunteer to break the news to him and try, tactfully, to find out why she might have felt driven to this?

The device we used to allow everyone to be involved in this was a one-way mirror. Those sitting in the circle would see and hear what was going on in the room, unknown to those in the 'room' (the middle of the circle). I took the role of father – who was obviously upset and confused, but aware that his daughter was unhappy because there had been a lot of family arguments.

This was a very exhausting, demanding and powerful session – initial giggles at the 'dead body' were quickly dispelled as pupils became involved in the experience. Later, groups reconstructed scenes from the dead girl's life and interviewed friends and relatives in order to build a picture of what her life was like. Subsequently, I asked pupils to produce 'The Reema Goraya File' which was to contain as much information as possible, in a variety of modes, and suggested some ideas. Items produced by pupils included extracts from Reema's diary, a newspaper account of her suicide, accounts or 'transcripts' of interviews, descriptions of her family life and her school report. I was also aware that the majority of the class now expected that Sumitra would commit suicide, which would be an interesting reference point for discussion after finishing the novel!

Reflection

At several points in the novel, Sumitra's inner turmoils are reflected in descriptions of dreams that she has – the penultimate page in the book being perhaps the most significant. Coming where it does, just before she leaves, this dream offered an ideal stimulus for reflection on the book and the meanings the pupils had made from it. The work would be more theatrical and stylised, but nonetheless seemed to offer rich potential for expressing ideas, responses, attitudes and feelings through a different form.

I split the class into groups of seven or eight and gave the brief that they were to find a way of presenting visually and with sound the dream Sumitra has on her first night after she has left home. I referred them to Sumitra's dreams, and suggested a few possibilities: characters who appear and speak to her; incidents from the past; her fantasies, etc. and left them to it. Each group would work using improvisation which would then lead to a script, and the final product was to be video-taped.

The results were remarkable. The dreams drew heavily on the actual text and there was much lively (and often heated) argument as to what should be included and how to present it effectively. From very humble beginnings with pair exercises, we had moved through emotional experience to a considered, polished, thoughtful and often moving theatrical presentation, which drew on the narrative but was not merely a re-enactment or replay of past events.

From the point of view of coursework pieces, the pupils presented the following:

1   Three invented dialogues using characters from the novel.
2   The Reema Goraya File.
3   A script and explanatory notes 'Sumitra's Dream'. (Some pupils presented this piece in narrative form, using the material from their presentation.)

The opportunities for oral assessment were also varied – though arriving at an actual assessment was more problematical. We were able to meet the following objectives specified in the syllabus:

• understand and convey information
• understand, order and present facts, opinions and ideas
• articulate experience and express what is felt and imagined

- articulate a response to the reading of a whole text
- sense of audience and style

Many of the assessments of pupils were made informally and on the spot, but the tape-recordings of pair and group work and the video of Sumitra's dream gave tangible evidence which could be discussed, moderated and used as evidence of the kinds of oral activities pupils had engaged in. The actual assessment itself and the procedures and standards become a focus for departmental discussion – and the tapes and videos enabled us to discuss exactly which criteria were being met and how to award grades – which in turn gave us confidence in making assessments in our own classrooms.

For example, in the pair work we were able to identify the following areas to assess:

- ability to describe and reflect upon experience within the context of task
- ability to recognise and respond to ideas and attitude expressed by a partner
- ability to use pace and tone in keeping with context
- ability to formulate questions and respond to the questions of others
- ability to use appropriate register and vocabulary to suit context
- ability to recognise needs of partner – a sense of audience
- ability to listen to and understand and respond to a partner's point of view

Significantly, because the talk was rooted in a combination of direct experience and indirect experience via the novel, it was sustained, purposeful and helped students to make their own sense not only of what they had read, but of other related issues. The written work grew out of a combination of drama, discussion and reading experiences, which had their roots in an understanding of the text, but allowed pupils to make their own meanings. G.C.S.E. responds to these needs by creating a certification system based upon meaningful experiences for pupils – and I'm sure that the written work produced was more thoughtful, reflective and genuinely personal than a remote task such as 'Write a character study of Sumitra'.

9

A Wizard of Earthsea – Ursula Le Guin

(A way in through drama)

This chapter gives an account of a project in which the various strategies described in this book were used to provide the pivot around which reading of a class novel, talking, listening and writing revolved.

The door bursts open and 2 JLB momentarily come to a halt. They have not met me before as I have just arrived back in school after a term's secondment. Warily they eye the English classroom – chairs and tables pushed back against the walls – this is not what they are used to. I have been advised that last term they were 'rather excitable and boisterous' and as they shuffle in I wonder if I should be 'doing drama' with them in this first session! I am an unknown quantity to them – they eye both me and the room quizzically.

We sit in a loose circle and I ask them what they think a School for Wizards would be like, what sort of people would go there, what kinds of things might happen there. Slowly the idea takes hold, comments and suggestions are shared. I ask them if they think they could try and create a wizard's school in the classroom – they are curious, and agree, somewhat tentatively. I say, 'I think it might help if you had some ideas about yourself before we start,' and the next fifteen minutes are spent jotting down a secret name, a special ability or power, a reason for coming, any skills or knowledge they have. We agree that people joining such a school would only have limited ability or perhaps just indications or hints of power, although one boy doggedly insists he can throw fireballs! I explain that we will start with the arrival of the apprentice wizards and sorcerers, and that I will play a role as well, and they move to one half of the classroom standing apart from each other. I stand in the other half of the room, between two chairs approximately six feet apart. My verbal organisation shifts imperceptibly into a narration:

'After a long and tiring journey you have finally arrived. As you move towards the gateway you become aware of others around you, arriving from different directions, until finally you are outside a large gateway,' I pause.

The group sense the reason and begin to converge on me . . .

Stepping out towards them I raise my hand and, in a quiet voice, ask,

'And why have you come to this place?'

Silence, punctuated by a few giggles.

'What is it you wish, strangers?'

Shuffling of feet, whispers, giggles . . . silence.

I stand my ground, calmly staring at them. I am just about to stop the drama and talk about it when a girl steps out . . .

'We've come to find the Wizard's School.' Mutters of agreement.

'We all search, only some of us find,' I reply enigmatically.

The class are confused, uncertain; my reply has been too oblique. Another girl steps forward. 'We've come a long way to learn how to be wizards. Can we come in?'

I decide not to continue the pressure yet. I move aside and gesture to the 'gate'.

'Enter apprentices – you are welcome, pass through if that is your desire.'

They do so, giving me a noticeably wide berth.

Altering my tone of voice and taking up teacher stance again I freeze the movement and continue to narrate the scene. Aloud, I wonder how the new apprentices feel, and ask several pupils to speak aloud (soliloquise) their thoughts or feelings in role, or to describe what they see.

'A pile of desks and a bookcase,' is the first reply – laughter. The second response is 'nothing,' but as I continue the responses change – 'A courtyard with people in funny clothes'; 'A cold stone building with no windows'; 'Who is that man at the gate?'; 'I thought I wasn't going to be allowed in'. There has been a definite shift in atmosphere, and the class have had to cope with a lot of new things.

I break the drama here – now is the time to think over what has happened and to allow them to build and develop the situation.

Importantly I have succeeded in two major aims: I have engaged their attention and they have begun to take on the idea of a wizard's school, and not once has anyone said, 'This is kid's stuff!'

The last time I had used *A Wizard of Earthsea* as a class reader had been a notable disaster! The class (also second years) complained endlessly – it was too difficult, it was boring, it was kid's stuff, the words and names were too hard, they couldn't follow the story. We had plodded on, but their initial suspicion of the subject matter hardened into resistance and unwillingness to become involved in the experience of the book. Part of the problem they had sensed for themselves – the subject matter, on the surface, of wizards and dragons and magic they classed as beneath them, yet the complex style, imagery and vocabulary was very adult. They became confused by the names, the details, and found it hard to follow the narrative thread. I decided to try again with the novel and face these problems head on. The book itself would become the cornerstone of our English work – around which we would build the writing, talking, listening and thinking activities.

The first hurdle to cross was that of the subject matter – if I could arouse and stimulate interest in that before introducing them to the book itself, if we could explore and build a similar atmosphere, then maybe I would not have the problems I did last time. The context I chose for the drama was broadly parallel to that of the book, but did not tie us to the book's plot. And it was a context that had certain key advantages – the class could bring to bear all their own experiences of starting a new school, weighing up other people, establishing themselves, and their roles as apprentice wizards, meeting my role as the Archmage, would be very close to the real situation of them meeting me for the first time! Since we would not be tied to a predetermined narrative line the direction of the drama could be negotiated, and it was important that early on in the work they had the opportunity for content, direction and form. I have already described how the first lesson began. The lesson continues . . .

They decide to call the school 'Raven's Rock' and arrange the space according to how they feel the Great Hall would look. I explain that they have now gathered in the Great Hall to await the Archmage, and we go back into the drama. I repeat the soliloquy exercise and narrate the scene, then enter the space in role as the Archmage, walking slowly up the Great Hall, turning and facing the apprentices who are ranged on three sides of the Hall. I introduce myself and welcome them briefly, and then approach each apprentice in turn, asking their name (we had already agreed their 'common' names would be their own when compiling backgrounds) enquiring about their special skill, ability, power or knowledge, commenting on it (elevating even the most simple answers to importance and value) and, as they respond to the questions, I hold their gaze, and formally shake each by the hand. Some find it difficult, and there are giggles at first, but this gradually subsides. (This lengthy session was important since it established for them and for the others who they each were, and committed each pupil to the seriousness of the situation and his/her role. The group in fact commented afterwards on how unnerving and difficult this section had been.)

I explain their first task – to meet me tomorrow and tell me what is the most important thing for a wizard to always remember! Then I leave the Great Hall, and deliberately stand back. Can they manage this without help? Pairs and small groups quickly form to talk over the Archmage's task, and one girl takes the lead and brings the suggestions together, firstly by going from group to group but then by calling everyone together to get agreement. She is appointed spokesperson to tell the Archmage . . . and we stop the drama there, to talk over what has happened. To consolidate the experience I ask them (for homework) to write a diary entry that night as they sit alone in their room, giving their thoughts, impressions, fears, hopes and reactions:

'My room is squalid – just a bare bed and stone chair. Today has been the most frightening day of my life, though I have met new friends. When I sighted the peak of Raven's Rock I was excited, but when I got there I saw people of different colours talking different languages. The meeting with the Archmage was nerve-racking – I don't feel very important, talking to fish is such a puny skill. But I hope to learn here . . .'

'What a mystery! I thought being here would increase my power – I'd like to look into the future like some of the others can. I'm a little frightened by the power of the Archmage, but I think I can learn from him. I wish I knew spells to tidy up the cobwebs in this room – it is really dirty – I'd have thought it'd be clean myself.'

'Today has been exciting and tiring – listening to everyone else's skills and talents made me realise that I have a lot to learn. I hope I get on with everyone – they all seem strange and to know what they're doing. I'll keep away from the one who can turn things to stone. I wonder if she can change people. Better not cross her!'

'My bedroom is simple, with only one window. The place gives me the creeps, especially the mountains looking forbiddingly down. The room is carved out of rock – I wonder if all the rooms are? I am very confused – I'm full of questions about this strange place and the Archmage. What is it I must remember? Always concentrate? Or work hard? I don't know what to say, I don't know the answer, if there really is an answer.'

Life at Raven's Rock was the theme of the next few sessions; deciphering scrolls covered with runic symbols (code-breaking); writing spells and chants and inventing secret runes to record them; still-images to show aspects of life at the school; pairs discussing their past and what they missed; groups making up and demonstrating new spells were among the activities covered.

It was during this time we embarked upon reading the book itself. They were eager and enthusiastic, the first hurdle was cleared! Two pieces of writing came out of the reading: they wrote their own stories describing how they first became aware that they had a special power or ability which were put into the Archives of Raven's Rock; and they also wrote a letter from Ogion introducing Ged to the Archmage of Roke Island School. I mention this latter task since it was a way of organising and clarifying their understanding of Ged's character – especially his impetuosity and pride. Little did I know that it would be used directly in a future drama lesson by one of the group!

I felt it vital that the Raven's Rock drama now took a new direction which would challenge them to deepen their engagement with the situation, and maybe move them towards the text itself. I considered confronting the apprentices as Archmage and accusing some of abusing or misusing their powers, or perhaps saying there was rivalry and jealousy . . . but, although it might have been useful to move more directly into the events of the book, I felt that the decision should be theirs – it was time for them to take control of the drama.

I interrupted the next session with 'Apprentices . . . the council of Elders has uncovered a serious problem, here, in Raven's Rock.' Deliberate pause, I eye them seriously . . . 'Never before has anything like this happened – it affects each of us . . .' At this point I break the drama and discuss with the group, out of role, what he might say, shifting it to what do you want him to say? Which is the most interesting problem to pursue in our drama? They decide that some of the apprentices are spies for an evil sorcerer. They quickly move on to suggest a form: I was secretly to appoint spies, and some of the group would be the Council who would examine the apprentices. The apprentices meanwhile will conduct unofficial enquiries. Unknown to them I added to this form – and our drama now had a new focus, new tensions, and specific contexts for specialised language use, as the Council interviewed all the apprentices, probing their backgrounds, trying to trick them, being devious or threatening, while the three spies set about trying to sound out and recruit two new members without arousing suspicion from the other apprentices!

At this time it felt appropriate to enter into the text itself through drama. They had absorbed the flavour of a wizard's school; their writing and talking had been sharpened by working in role; they had experienced a problem and faced it; they had begun to take initiatives and consider form; they were involved with the book itself. I wanted the next phase of the work to move directly into the situations and characters of the book. Discussion and writing during our reading had shown understanding of Ged's character, but some of the group were still finding it difficult to hold everything together in their heads, or were merely absorbing the storyline without thinking beyond it.

We had just finished reading 'The Loosing of the Shadow', and I wanted to try to establish more clearly the nature of the Shadow, since it is crucial to the way the story develops, and to get the group to consider the way in which this affects Ged. Through drama I hoped to help the group consolidate all they had picked up about character, motivation and relationships so far, and to encourage them not only to remember the narrative thread and key incidents but to interpret why things were happening and consider implications. By comparing their own ideas of what might happen with what the author decides to make happen they would also become aware of the range of choices facing an author.

To 'act out' the events leading to the 'Loosing of the Shadow' would, to my mind, add nothing. What is important is to understand *why* – and to be inside a fictional situation requiring empathy, hypothesis, recall, and interpretation of the text, will not only throw the pupils back upon the book but require them to use their own experiences to articulate this understanding.

I decided to use the form they had already successfully handled in the Raven's Rock drama – an enquiry. This form would also enable the pupils to grapple with differing kinds of spoken language – explaining, justifying, defending, challenging, questioning, reporting. Questioning a character in role would throw the children directly back to the text – not only for literal understanding, but more importantly they would have to read between the lines of the narrative – to infer and deduce. However, I was not sure that anyone in 2JLB was ready or able to cope with this pressure alone. I decided to use 'corporate characters' with two or three pupils representing a single character.

Three pupils each represented a corporate Ged, Vetch, Jasper and Master Summoner, while the rest of the class were split into four groups of Council Elders who had to interview a character, establish the facts and decide what (if anything) should be done. After allocating roles, I organised the proceedings in role as Secretary to the Council, explaining that the Council would reconvene shortly to consider its findings. This role enabled me to step back from the centre of the proceedings – I could advise the Council over procedure if asked, or I could ask for an idea to be explained more fully so that I could document it. I could liaise between groups, pass messages, support and advise both sides, and yet I could also hand over initiative to the group themselves, and make them responsible for organisation and form, especially in the full Council Meeting. The class quickly and easily moved into the drama, drawing upon both the book and their experiences of the Raven's Rock drama, and the interviews were sharp and serious, the questions demanding and challenging, the answers thoughtful and deliberate, as each character was probed to get at the truth. Vetch was unwilling to apportion blame, Ged and Jasper gave very differing accounts, and the Master Summoner offered detailed warnings about the evil creature that was now in the world.

When the Council reconvened there was spirited argument as to who was to blame, and in order to clarify some of the discrepancies or fill in omissions other apprentices who witnessed the argument, the challenge and the summoning had to be called to give their versions. One Council Elder produced Ogion's letter (a previous piece of writing) and read it to the Council; reminding them that Ged was, and always had been, a 'show-off', he angrily demanded Ged should be punished – and was fiercely opposed by a girl who pointed out that Jasper always looked down on people, making snide comments and sarcastic remarks, and that we could not punish one without the other. 'Anyway,' she added, 'I bet you can't tell us you've never lost your temper.'

The wrangling continued, and they began to decide that both should be humbled, when I asked the Council to hear from the Master Summoner. (During the questioning session I had been impressed by the ideas he expressed about the nature of the Shadow, and hoped to introduce a new focus and tension into the meeting by using this. I was prepared to support him using my secretary role.)

The Master Summoner explained he had spent all last night watching for the return of the Shadow – the Archmage had not killed it – it was loose in the world. I pressed him to explain why this was important, and how it affected us here in Roke; he replied that it was waiting out there to destroy us with its evil, it was a nameless thing from hell that had escaped. (I was most impressed by this boy's recall of the events and information. I had deliberately chosen to have the Master Summoner interviewed in order that this possibility could arise – manipulative perhaps, but it was the Shadow I wanted to explore!)

I turned to the Council and suggested we meet again tomorrow, in the meantime each was to consult his/her books of lore to see what information could be found about the nature of this evil thing.

We broke the drama there, and I explained that they would have to invent this information – we discussed the forms it might take – fragments of legends, diary extracts, passing references in books of spells and lore, descriptions in books of curses, entries in dictionaries of evil, and the written pieces that came back to the next Council meeting were remarkable for their authentic look and style. The following example actually formed the basis of the drama which now was to develop:

'Ye olde black beaste cometh from ye worlde beyond. It is summoned when the dead be falsely called. It's claws like blades rip and tear and destroy human flesh of those it detestes and those who summon the beast.

It has no body, claws and fangs used only for destruction.

Note well, there is but one known way to banish the beast – all Master Summoners must be gathered together then the beast be summoned once it is come, their joint strength will defeat the beast for all time.

Take heed, other beastes may well follow the same deadly
path . . .'

. . . and the drama moved back out of the narrative line of the text,
as they explored ways of dealing with the Shadow – ultimately
summoning it and defeating it. Although we had moved away from
the text, our own experiences and understanding of the Shadow
were tested and compared against information that we discovered in
subsequent reading – and although the Shadow was dealt with in our
drama, they were, during reading, intrigued and eager to find out
how Ged would deal with it.

Perhaps the class themselves should have the final say. These are
just a few of many similar comments:

'Our own drama called Raven's Rock helped me believe the book
and feel more into the place.'

'The drama has made the book more interesting and gets you
involved.'

'I have now understood the parts in the book which are more
complicated. It makes the book more exciting – you have to think up
ideas which you don't have to if you just read the book.'

'When we read the book it was a bit confusing and I got muddled
up with the characters, but when we do drama with the book, you
seem to get what the story's all about.'

'The drama helps me work the book out, but it is hard to believe in
it.'

'The book is exciting even though I find it hard to understand the
hard words and long sentences – but the drama work has helped me
understand it a bit more – especially trying to work out what was in
someone's mind was really hard but now I get it.'

10

Where Now?

In this book my aim has been to share ways of working that I have found to be both successful and worthwhile, and I hope that readers will find things to both try out and to think about. Some of the ideas can be tried out immediately, but are offered not as handy lesson plans but in order to suggest in practical terms how a range of drama strategies might enrich the learning experiences offered to pupils. Once you have gained confidence in working in role, and are at ease with these ways of working in the classroom, the next stage is to adapt the strategies to suit your own situation and needs.

Many of the lesson frameworks and accounts that have been described offer structured ways of beginning this type of work, but it is not always as simple as I may have made it sound. The important thing is to have a go, and find what works for you and your pupils.

Working space

All of the examples described in this book have been successfully used in ordinary classrooms. Space is created by stacking the desks around the sides of the room, leaving room to arrange chairs in a large circle, or groups. Once a class knows the routine, this can be done very quickly and quietly, but be clear about simple rules for safety and keeping the noise level down.

Working in a classroom means you can easily switch between drama, discussion, reading, writing, research, etc. and have access to any equipment and resources necessary. Though a drama studio, or hall, can give space and freedom to engage in activities without fear of disturbing others, pupils do have preconceptions about working in such areas; if something isn't working it's easier to switch perspective, or move into writing or drawing if you are in the classroom. It also means you can incorporate drama activities for just part of a lesson with minimum disruption.

Discipline

There may well be times when the noise level is unacceptable, the work is superficial (or even silly), the pupils are play-acting, not being serious or not concentrating. It is vital from the start that the rules are made clear and that for the work to achieve anything everyone understands that we *all* have to work at it together.

Sometimes disruption can be tackled in role (do you wish to leave the Council Chamber? . . . Is this how we react to our Queen? . . . Can you do this important task for us?) but it is important to stop the work if necessary and discuss what is happening. Drama demands that participants trust and respect each other, and power-coercive approaches tend to be counter-productive (though I have, occasionally had to stop the drama and speak quite severely to persistent disrupters). The onus is upon *us* – teacher(s) and students – to make this work. If it is to work we need to try and be serious. Talking about the work, ('it's sometimes hard not to giggle isn't it? Why is this do you think? . . . Do you think the villagers would really respond like this?) with the emphasis on how it can be made to work and *feel right* is crucial, and may need considerable time. If the pupils feel the work is theirs and have a say in decisions, then the work becomes important to them, and the drama provides its own discipline.

Working in role for the first time can present problems for a class who are not used to interacting with you in this way, so in the early stages of such work keep the teacher role straightforward (e.g. as in the 'Mystery Document' described in Chapter 2). Chapter 1 outlined some ways of beginning to work in role, and again, if necessary stop the drama if something is not working, and talk it through with the class. ('Did it feel right? Did it sound right? How could we do this differently? How do you feel when I speak to you as someone else? Is it a problem?)

Generally I tend to avoid the term 'drama', especially in the early stages of establishing working patterns and routines – and use the word 'role-play' which doesn't carry the same connotations or preconceptions!

Getting started

Looking back over the various lessons – which ones seem to hold immediate appeal? What would you need to do to try to adapt one to suit you? The 'H.D. Factor' (Chapter 2) is a safe, structured way in, and need only occupy one lesson. Perhaps you could take the novel your class is currently reading. Is there a character who could be hot-seated? Are there any key moments that could be frozen into still-images, and then characters questioned about feelings and motives? These activities are relatively simple to organise and need only occupy part of a lesson. Have a go at 'The Mystery Document' – using the materials provided (it isn't necessary to use the lesson as a way-in to *A Question of Courage*). Better still, why not adapt the framework to fit something your class is reading or working on at present – all it needs is a bit of preparation, which could be done in collaboration with a colleague, using the structure to fit round your own 'archive' material.

Alternatively, why not adapt one of the frameworks and tailor it to fit in with your own and your pupils' interests and needs. What issue or learning area do you want to explore? What roles could the pupils be cast in to explore the situation, and what context will they operate in: 'experts' called in to advise, villagers discussing a new development before attending a public meeting; people giving evidence to an inquiry?

It is important to remember that time is needed to develop this kind of work, and not to have too high an expectation or an over-ambitious plan. You will be learning about what works as you evaluate and reflect upon sessions, but be flexible and don't stick rigidly to a plan if it doesn't seem to be working, or the pupils decide on a new focus.

Working collaboratively

Talking about your work and sharing it with colleagues has enormous benefits (in both ideas and support). I have found working with colleagues in classrooms, observing each others' lessons, planning frameworks together and sharing problems and ideas has helped me considerably to understand more about the complex processes in a classroom.

Why not ask a colleague to help out? Perhaps they could be a character in a novel whom the class hot-seat, or they could take on the role of Mr/s King in 'The H.D. Factor'. Or they could even just talk through some ideas or share thoughts about a lesson. Or, as in the lessons on *Lord of the Flies*, you could collaborate with a colleague on a novel – planning some work and evaluating it together afterwards. The teaching could be conducted separately and the responses of two different classes explored.

Departmental workshops, meetings or INSET sessions could have some of the ideas in this book on an agenda, so that a range of experiences can contribute to any developments or trying out of approaches. A lesson framework can be critically discussed, and alternative structures or adaptations can be explored. After some teaching, the responses can be brought back for the department to explore (short tape transcripts may be useful for looking at language skills in operation as a way of providing a focus).

External support

As well as enlisting the help, advice, encouragement and support of colleagues (and don't forget the drama department or specialist drama teachers if you have them), external agencies are another useful resource to draw upon. In my experience English and/or drama advisory teachers are more than willing to come into school and work alongside individuals or even departments. Such arrangements need careful planning, and need to be scheduled well in advance, but can offer fresh practical insight and support for the kind of work described in this book. Advisory teachers may be willing (as they are in my authority) to come in for an intensive few days, or a series of smaller time-slots (e.g. Periods 1 and 2 each Thursday for a month).

To gain the most from such external support, it will be important to try to make time so that as well as sharing the teaching you can meet before and after sessions to plan and evaluate. In this context, it is advisable to seek INSET time, but even ad hoc visits and joint teaching are an invaluable resource. Depending upon the advisory networks available (and your access to the people within them), you may be able to contact colleagues in local schools or ask for school- or centre-based INSET. There are a number of authorities who have mounted excellent INSET provision (both in schools and centres), and it is important to remember to contact both your English and your drama advisory service, as these are sometimes separate entities.

Finding material

There is no difference between the ways in which you find material for this kind of work and the ways in which you find material for your other English work; what is different is how you approach and use the material. Literature is of course one of our richest resources – as well as novels and stories, poems also lend themselves to active explorations through drama.

A narrative poem such as 'Flannan Isle' could be approached in several ways. Perhaps the class are villagers living in the local community invaded by reporters. Maybe some are related to the missing lighthouse keepers? Alternatively they could be lighthouse commissioners convening a court of inquiry or researchers working for a supernatural phenomena magazine. Pupils could recreate in still-images the events surrounding the disappearance (and invent their own explanations), or contact the missing men through a spiritualist medium who can only answer their questions with knocks to signify yes or no.

The same kinds of strategies can be applied to play-texts or films. If a class in role as Time-Life reporters interview people (including Arthur Miller) and research and reconstruct events during McCarthyism in the 1950s, how do they perceive *The Crucible* when they subsequently explore, as historians and archivists, the events and characters in the play? How would a court of inquiry apportion blame for the deaths of Romeo and Juliet? What stories would servants tell of the events in Dunsinane Castle at various stages of Macbeth?

Pictures can also provide interesting starting points: who are these people; what are they thinking? Groups can reconstruct a series of still-images leading up to this picture. What kind of life would we lead in this type of area? What would happen if we brought this scene to life? Who would we be if we lived here? Pictures provide a concrete starting point from which pupils can explore ideas, themes and situations that they have some control over.

Contemporary news items and newspaper articles are another rich source of stimulus material (even advertisements – 'Haunt-Away' stemmed from a local bus company's publicity leaflet posted through my door!). Here pupils can begin to explore the human realities behind the news, and sort out their own feelings by considering a range of perspectives. I was asked recently to take part in the school's 'Aids Education' programme for fifth years. In role as teachers we considered the implications of the news that one of our haemophiliac pupils had contracted the virus and was now HIV positive. This was set against being groups of parents who had heard rumours about the news and culminated in a parent-teacher meeting (at which the biology teacher was in role as a doctor). This was interspersed with pupils talking as pupils about the rumours, pairs/threes discussing issues as staff and much discussion out of role.

Theory into practice

Essentially I can only try and share what I have found to be a challenging and rewarding approach that forms a part of my English teaching. Everything I claim here is open to modification in the light of your own experience. The theory that underpins the practice grows from the practice, but any theory of educational action is hypothetical: it is provisional and subject to revision by being tested in the classroom. I hope the frameworks, and especially the case studies offer a comparative context against which to judge better your own values and the learning taking place in your classroom. By testing, refining and elaborating the approaches (and the underpinning theory) new theories and approaches will be generated, and like our pupils, we become active meaning makers. As Stenhouse says in *An Introduction to Curriculum Research and Development*, 'there is no mastery, only aspiration'; we too are constantly learning and finding ways to enhance the quality of the learning taking place in our classrooms.

Novels referred to

(The editions referred to are those I use in school.)

Across the Barricades, Joan Lingard (Penguin Plus, 1988)
The second book about the relationship between a Catholic boy
and a Protestant girl in Belfast. Although part of a series, it stands
on its own. (13+) See Chapter 5.

Annerton Pit, Peter Dickinson (Heinemann Windmills, 1978)
A story that shifts between the 'supernatural' and reality,
combining elements of thriller, adventure, mystery and
supernatural stories. The main character is blind which gives the
narrative an unusual orientation. (14+) See Chapter 6.

Brother in the Land, Robert Swindells (Penguin Plus, 1985)
Life after the nuclear holocaust – a boy and a girl discover harsh
realities in a world where old values no longer apply. Extremely
powerful with a compelling narrative line. 1984 Children's
Book Award Winner. (14+) See Chapter 6.

Buddy, Nigel Hinton (Heinemann Windmills, 1983)
Buddy has to face his own feelings when his parents split up and
his dad appears to be drifting into crime. Woven into this plot is an
exploration by Buddy and two friends of an empty house where a
murder was committed, making an exciting but thought-
provoking story. (Good for 13+) See Chapters 6 and 7.

Carrie's War, Nina Bawden (Heinemann Windmills, 1975)
Set against the background of the evacuation of children during
World War II this is both an exciting and sensitive story. The
characterisation is especially effective, particularly of Carrie
herself. (12+) See Chapter 4.

Day of the Triffids, John Wyndham (Hutchinson Unicorn)
A classic science fiction story of the future, and of survival, which
still grips students. (Interesting to set against *Brother in the
Land*). (14+) See Chapter 7.

Dragonslayer, Rosemary Sutcliffe (Puffin, 1966)
The story of Beowolf re-told in lively and evocative language. The
strong narrative line makes the story accessible to younger
readers. (11+) See Chapters 1 and 2.

Eleanor, Elizabeth, Libby Gleeson (Puffin, 1986)
Eleanor's family move to the Australian outback and Eleanor has
to learn about herself, cope with a new school and understand an

alien environment. A mixture of fantasy and adventure, the story works on several levels. (12+) Highly commended in 1984 Australian Children's Book Awards. See Chapter 7.

Escape!, Roberta Kehle (Lion, 1984)
The story of a family who have to leave their home in war-torn Laos, their journey to a refugee camp, life in the camp and finally settlement in America. Despite some political stereotyping, the novel deals with the experiences extremely sensitively, and makes people seen in the news more real. (11+) See Chapter 7.

Frankenstein's Aunt, Allan Rune Pettersson (Heinemann Windmills, 1982)
The monster is re-awakened by Aunt Frankenstein, determined to restore the family's good name! Enter a Werewolf and Count Dracula . . . a lively, imaginative and funny story! (11+) See Chapters 1 and 5.

A Game of Soldiers, Jan Needle (Fontana Lions, 1985)
Three children find a wounded Argentinian conscript during the Falklands crisis. Games are now real, and attitudes and values have to be confronted. Provocative and challenging issues, in a story that is easy to read. (11+) See Chapter 6.

The Green Leaves of Nottingham, Pat McGrath (Hutchinson Unicorns, 1973)
The harsh realities of teenagers growing up against a background of delinquency and deprivation are convincingly portrayed – the novel pulls no punches! (14+) See Chapter 7.

A Kestrel for a Knave, Barry Hines (Arnold Wheaton, 1969)
There is still a lot in this book, and students both identify with the context and are moved by the situation of Billy, his family, and his hawk. (14+) See Chapter 6.

Lord of the Flies, William Golding (Faber, 1954)
Quite interesting to set alongside *Brother in the Land* to explore views of human nature. Difficult, but still raises many issues. (14+) See Chapters 5, 6 and 7.

The Mayor of Casterbridge, Thomas Hardy (Penguin)
Despite its massive size, more able students readily involve themselves in this. (15+) See Chapter 5.

Of Mice and Men, John Steinbeck (Heinemann Windmills)
Never fails to provoke responses! (13+) See Chapters 5 and 6.

A Question of Courage, Marjorie Darke (Fontana Lions, 1978)
Two young women search for their identities in a society that has

135

rigid expectations of their roles and responsibilities. Though from very different backgrounds their involvement in the suffragette cause unites them. An excellent novel, though the ending drifts into romanticism! (13+) See Chapter 2.

The Scarecrows, Robert Westall (Heinemann Windmills, 1984)
A disturbingly haunting story of a boy's attempts to come to grips with new family relationships, as the supernatural world and the real world intertwine. Rivetting and quite complex, working on many levels. (14+) See Chapter 7.

The Silver Sword, Ian Serraillier (Heinemann Windmills)
Continues to be popular – combining fast-paced narrative with more serious issues. (11+). See Chapter 7.

Sumitra's Story, Rukshana Smith (Bodley Head, 1982)
Sumitra's family have to leave Uganda and settle in Britain, but Sumitra increasingly finds herself torn between two cultures she is unable to reconcile, while also searching for a sense of identity as a woman. This book challenges and confronts many issues, and was the winner of the 1982 Garavi Gujarat Book Award for Racial Harmony. (14+) See Chapter 8.

Walkabout, James Vance Marshall (Heinemann Windmills, 1977)
This story of two white children's relationship with an aboriginal boy when they are stranded in the outback continues to prove popular and the ideas are very accessible across the ability range. (13+) See Chapter 7.

Welcome Home, Jellybean, Marlene Fanta Shyer (Collins Cascade, 1984)
Neil's sister is mentally handicapped – and for the past thirteen years has been in state care. Then the family brings her home . . . a very moving story, which deals with the traumas and complexities of emotional turmoil in a family. (14+) See Chapters 6 and 7.

The White Mountains, John Christopher (Hutchinson Unicorns, 1974)
The world is ruled by mysterious Tripods. Young people are 'capped' and become docile adults. Three boys escape being capped, and travel in search of safety in the White Mountains . . . interesting perspective on modern civilisation and some solid science fiction creatures. Recently serialised on BBC1. Two excellent sequels. (12+) See Chapters 1 and 7.

A Wizard of Earthsea, Ursula Le Guin (Heinemann Windmills, 1973)
The first part of a fantasy trilogy, but it stands on its own. Ged the young wizard is eager to prove his skills in the wizard's school –

but summons a nameless evil. Complex language, but a fast-moving story. (12+) See Chapter 9.

Z for Zachariah, Robert O'Brien (Heinemann Windmills, 1976)
A teenage girl thinks she is the only survivor of a nuclear war, until a stranger appears in her valley. Told in diary form, the novel raises many moral issues as it builds to a shocking, disturbing climax. (14+) See Chapter 2.

1984, George Orwell (Penguin, 1954)
This nightmare vision of the future is as powerful and relevant today as it was when it was written. (15+) See Chapter 8.